The Wonderful World of Christmas Trees

The Wonderful World of Christmas Trees

THE WONDERFUL WORLD OF CHRISTMAS TREES

By Henry H. Albers and Ann Kirk Davis

Mid-Prairie Books / Parkersburg, Iowa

First Edition

ISBN 0-931209-69-2

Library of Congress Catalog Card Number 97-73829

Photo credits: cover photographs of growing Christmas trees and decorated
tree with candles, courtesy of the National Christmas Tree Association
and Colonial Williamsburg Foundation

Design and Printing: Woolverton Printing

To Paul Ridgway Kirk, Sr.

CONTENTS

PREFACE

INTRODUCTION

THE BEGINNING IN STRASBOURG

A Time for Christmas 3

A Christmas Tree in Strasbourg 4

A European Tradition 6

Christmas Trees Come to North America 9

A FOCUS ON THE PIONEERS

Christmas Tree Markets.. 17

Pioneers Who Built an Industry 18

Christmas Trees are Banned 24

Christmas Tree Plantations 25

Beyond the Early Pioneers 31

The Christmas Tree Industry 33

CHRISTMAS TREE FORESTS AND FARMS

Improving upon Nature 35

Growing Quality Christmas Trees.................................. 38

Christmas Tree Species in North America 46

Christmas Trees are Environmentally Friendly 46

Choose and Cut Christmas Tree Farms 51

Christmas Tree Farming in Europe 55

CHRISTMAS TREES IN GLAMOROUS ATTIRE

At Home for Christmas 61

In Worldwide Views 65

Colonial Williamsburg... 71

A Crown Center Tree That Grows Ornaments 74

The National Christmas Tree.. 76

White House Trees 77

State Capitols and Mansions Light Their Trees 80

Trees for Mansions 82

MAP SHOWING MAJOR GROWING AREAS 47

CHRISTMAS TREE SPECIES IN NORTH AMERICA 87

AMERICAN AND CANADIAN INDUSTRY LEADERSHIP 88

PICTURE CREDITS.. 89

NOTES 90

SELECT BIBLIOGRAPHY 94

INDEX.. 96

PREFACE

It began with the writing of a brief history to accompany a display of Christmas trees at the Herbert Hoover Presidential Library & Museum, West Branch, Iowa. The research led to a preliminary plan for a possible book. After exploring various alternatives, a decision was made to limit the subject matter to real trees as opposed to artificial trees. Real trees include trees that are cut and living trees in nature or containers destined to be decorated for Christmas. It was also decided to give comprehensive consideration to the growing of Christmas trees and to tell much of the story in photographs.

At this point the problem of obtaining data and photographs on growing Christmas trees began to create uncertainties about the project. Fortunately, Bob Scott, the President of the National Christmas Tree Association, suggested someone who could not only help but make a major contribution as a co-author. This person began her sojourn with Christmas trees as a family member of one of the largest companies in the industry. The importance of her expertise and experience, and personal contact with people in the industry cannot be overestimated.

We reviewed the originally proposed content and decided to give comprehensive consideration to the pioneers of the industry with photographs from family archives. The final product is capsuled in the INTRODUCTION of the book.

Two authors involve some kind of division of labor. The various responsibilities such as writing the narrative, gathering photographs, providing background information and data, and editorial responsibilities were not always equally divided. The important consideration is that we are happy with our respective contributions and cooperative endeavors. Both of us have concluded that without the other this book would not have been possible.

Literally hundreds of people have helped in many ways and we cannot thank them all. Our appreciation and thanks are extended to those listed in the sections on INDUSTRY OFFICIALS AND DIRECTORS, PICTURE CREDITS, and NOTES in the back portion of the book. We would like to give a special word of thanks to the following individuals: Paul "Rick" Kirk, Jr., President of the Kirk Company, for reviewing major portions of the manuscript and providing a large number of photographs; Joan Geiger, Associate Executive Director, National Christmas Tree Association, Inc. for her help in obtaining photographs and in other innumerable ways; Hella Roth of Inter Nationes, Bonn, Germany, for making available rare European photographs; Marjorie Albers for her help in editing and reviewing the manuscript; Daniel R. Jensen and Robert J. Swiatly for designing the layout; and Robert Neymeyer, our publisher, for his many helpful suggestions and support.

Henry H. Albers   Ann Kirk Davis

INTRODUCTION

This book has dimensions in time and space that go far beyond the Christmas season. A creative combination of colorful pictures and narrative portrays the wonderful world of evergreen trees both before and after they are dressed in ornaments and glowing lights. Beginning as small seedlings, the trees require years of loving care before they become Christmas trees. The creative talents of the pioneers and the people who work all year to make it happen are given center stage. At Christmas time the greenery and fragrance of the trees cast a magic spell.

From the privacy of the home and the sanctity of the church, Christmas trees have moved into every sphere of human activity. They are found in national and state capitols, city halls and squares, ships at sea, historic houses and mansions, universities, and business enterprises. They have reached across ethnic boundaries to become a symbol of unity among people, including those who are not Christian or religious.

The wonderful world of Christmas trees is introduced with German color lithographs from centuries past. Photographs from family archives reflect upon the "good old days" of the pioneers of more recent years. Beautiful natural settings in full color show people doing interesting work to create beautifully shaped trees. The scene then turns to trees in special places after they are decorated for the holidays. Christmas trees are truly up-front all year long.

Christmas Eve at the Wandsbeker Castle, 1796, a color engraving by Hugo Burkner. Courtesy Inter Nationes

THE BEGINNING IN STRASBOURG

The display of evergreen dates back to the early Egyptians, Hebrews, Druids, and Persians, almost from the beginning of Biblical time. Romans adorned their homes with greenery during the winter celebration of saturnalia to honor the god of agriculture, *Saturnus*. For pagan people in northern Europe decorations with greenery expressed a renewal of life during the darkness of winter. The winter solstice was also a time for celebration. Bonfires gave the winter god strength to hasten the return of light. The festivities honored pagan gods and not infrequently debauchery and drunkenness made them even more festive.

A Time for Christmas

In A.D. 440, lacking a historical date for the birth of Christ, church fathers upstaged the pagans by setting the date of the winter solstice as the time to celebrate Christmas. Calendars changed and so did the date of Christmas. In the Gregorian calendar, the winter solstice occurs on December 22 and most Christians celebrate Christmas on the 25th.[1]

Pagan Customs Bring Christmas Cheer

For several centuries throughout much of Christendom the celebration of Christmas was primarily observed by religious services. As pagans were converted to Christianity by words or swords, many festivities of the winter solstice became a part of Christmas festivities. Pope Gregory I specifically sanctioned this development in A.D. 601. His instructions to missionaries among the pagans read, "because they have been used to slaughter many oxen in the sacrifices to devils, some solemnity must be exchanged for them on this account . . . to the end that, whilst some gratifications are outwardly permitted them, they may the more easily consent to the inward consolations of the grace of God."[2]

This expression of papal tolerance was not without limitations. During the centuries that followed, bishops periodically banned the decorating of homes with evergreen as a pagan practice. People ignored them and continued to do so. A tree specifically identified as a Christmas tree did not appear until much later in spite of legends to the contrary.

A Christmas Tree for a Pagan Chieftain

Near the town of Fritzlar in the present-day German state of Hesse, there stood the sacred oak tree of the pagan god Donar, a site for human sacrifices. Upon hearing that the eldest son of the Chieftain Gundhar was to be sacrificed on Christmas Eve, Saint Boniface, an English born cleric, arrived with ax in hand and felled the giant oak. The throng who witnessed this act of defiance against a pagan god flocked to be baptized. Legend has it that a little fir tree sprang up to replace Donar's oak, and to add insult to injury, was cut and displayed in Gundhar's great hall to celebrate Christmas.

The Paradise Tree

During the middle ages, the church had problems teaching the moral lessons of the Bible in the face of illiteracy and a lack of printed books. Passion plays provided a way. During Advent, the four weeks preceding Christmas, the feature attraction was a play about Adam and Eve that began with their eviction from the Garden of Eden. The horrors of damnation and hellfire were vividly described. All ended well with the promise of salvation through the birth of Christ. A prop was the Paradise tree, an evergreen decorated with apples that symbolized the fruit of the forbidden tree, a precursor of the Christmas tree.

The Mythical Tree of Martin Luther

On a walk alone at night Martin Luther saw the beauty of bright stars shining through the evergreens in the forest. To show his children the beauty he had seen, Luther placed candles on a small evergreen tree outside the door and created a Christmas tree. A painting by artist Carl Schwerdgeburth in 1845 showed Luther and family around a candle-lit Christmas tree. The picture and popular belief have almost turned this legend into a historical fact. Otto Lauffer, the leading German authority on the subject, categorized the Luther story as pure myth.[3]

A Divine Origin

A German fairy tale tells the story of a forester, his wife, and two children who lived in a tiny cottage located deep in a forest. One night during a blizzard there was a knock on the door. Standing outside was a small boy who asked for shelter. "Yes," they said, "come in and stay with us." The family shared its meager food supply with the child, gave him clean clothing, and a warm bed. In the morning the family awoke to heavenly music and saw the young guest in radiant attire. "I am the Child Jesus," he said, "I want to show my appreciation for the kindness you have shown me with a gift for your Christmas celebration." He broke a twig from a fir tree and instantly there appeared a beautifully decorated Christmas tree.

A Christmas Tree in Strasbourg

A journal written in 1605 by a traveler reported that "at Christmas, people in Strasbourg set up fir trees in their rooms with roses cut from multicolored paper, apples, cakes, tinsel, and sugar hanging from the branches."[4] The first description of a decorated Christmas tree, but not the first Christmas tree. At this time Strasbourg was German in language and customs.

Ninety-foot Christmas tree in Kleber Square, Strasbourg, Alsace, France, where the first decorated tree was reported in 1605. Photo LAEMMEL/Ville de Strasbourg

No Trees More Than Eight Feet Tall

Christmas trees had been cut in the forests around Strasbourg as early as the 1500's and most likely some of these trees were decorated. A market for trees was present in 1539 and soon the cutting of fir trees began to play havoc with forests. By 1561, a forest ordinance in Ammerschweier limited the size of the trees that could be cut for Christmas to eight feet.[5]

Decorations and Wax Candles

By 1642, the custom of decorating trees had become so popular in Strasbourg that a minister, Johann Konrad Dannhauer, complained that "among the trifles to which people often devote more attention than the Word of God in celebrating the old Christmas is the Christmas or fir tree, which is set up at home, hung with dolls and sweets, and finally ransacked."[6] Candles were first mentioned by Lieselotte von der Pfalz, the Duchess of Orleans, in 1708 when she wrote that during her childhood in Germany fifty years earlier, boxwood trees were placed on tables with candles fixed to each branch.

Christmas trees decorated with wax candles had become more common by the 18th century. Professor Kissling of the university city of Wittenburg reported that in 1737 a woman had candle-lit Christmas trees for her children. The novel, *The Sorrows of Young Werther*, written by Goethe in 1774, describes a Christmas tree decorated by the heroine Lotte with sweets and apples and lighted with wax candles. Writing about her travels in 1785, the Baronin von Oberkirch observed that every house has a Christmas tree bedecked with lights and sweets. A few years later, Schiller described a tree in Ludwigsburg with wax candles and decorated with nuts, gingerbread, and sweets. By this time Christmas trees were known throughout Germany, more so in urban than rural areas.

Christmas morning, 1790. Copperplate etching by Josef Kelbner from a Swiss booklet for children. Courtesy Inter Nationes

A Religious Symbol

Legends and myths made the Christmas tree more acceptable as a Christian symbol. Protestant churches were the first to give approval, undoubtedly prompted by the Luther myth. The Catholic church gradually relented in its opposition and used the name, *Christbaum*, to remove the stigma of paganism. More secular names are *Weihnachtsbaum* and *Tannenbaum* and, in low German, the word is *Dannenboom*. Less frequently people speak of the *Lichterbaum* (tree of lights) and the widespread use of sweets as decorations created the name, *Zuckerbaum* (sugar tree).

Gift giving on Christmas Eve. Color wood engraving by Knilling, 1870. Courtesy Inter Nationes

"Today everything has changed! A tree must glitter and sparkle. Countless little ornaments turn the tree into a fairyland."[7]

Then Came Silver Tinsel

The glass industry in the Thuringia region of Germany discovered a new way of blowing glass ornaments with silver coating on the inside surface. Silver tinsel was produced from tinfoil and angels' hair, spangles, and silver stars from glass fiber. In 1893, *Gartenlaube*, a magazine for women, exclaimed:

Christmas Trees Without Decorations

Evergreen trees could be called Christmas trees only after they became a part of Christmas festivities. Trees that might have been present in pagan festivities of the winter solstice cannot properly be called Christmas trees. The same holds true for the Paradise tree that symbolized the fruit of the forbidden tree of the Book of Genesis, not the birth of Christ. The fir tree of Saint Boniface was a myth as was the candle-lit tree of Martin Luther.

In much of the literature a fir tree does not become a Christmas tree until it is decorated. This definition might be given a new dimension by including the millions of evergreen trees grown as Christmas trees. Carefully nurtured for many years, these trees are given an appropriate shape through pruning and shearing and cut shortly before Christmas to be decorated.

Beautiful Christmas trees without decorations.
Courtesy National Christmas Tree Association

A European Tradition

An Abundance of German Trees

Christmas trees are found in great abundance in German airports, railway stations, town squares, factories, offices, stores, churches, and schools. All of the major cities, Frankfurt, Hamburg, Munich, Nuremberg, and Berlin have elaborate displays of decorated trees, some of which attract tourists from many parts of the world. Even more important is the role of the Christmas tree in the home. The tree is hidden away from the children until it appears in all of its glory usually during the evening of December 24. It remains for a week or more to the delight of family and friends. In most German homes the decorated tree stands upright on the floor or a table. A few are hung from the ceiling which was originally done to take advantage of the mystical power of greenery to protect the house.

German Christmas trees are decorated in many different ways depending on family and community preferences. Some families trim their trees in the manner of earlier times with apples, nuts, sweets, and even pickles.

Nuts are often painted silver, gold, or dipped in sugar to make them more attractive. Other families choose hand-blown or machine-made glass ornaments, carved wooden and wax figures, silver plated stars and icicles, and brightly colored paper and tinsel. In spite of the less hazardous electric lights, many German families still prefer candles, especially those made from beeswax with their pleasant aroma.

Christmas tree decorations.
Colored lithograph from 1890.
Courtesy Inter Nationes

Decorating the Christmas tree. Lithograph of a drawing by Beyschlag, 1892.
Courtesy Inter Nationes

The Christmas tree of the Evangelical Lutheran Church in Nienstedten, a prestigious suburb of Hamburg, is still lighted with candles and decorated with baubles of various colors, small gifts, bells, and angel hair. Parishioners keep watch over the burning candles and tend to the ones that could start a fire. In the German community of Cole Camp, Missouri, this task was given to two men who stood in front of the pulpit with wet rags on a long pole and buckets of water. A Christmas tree is still hung from the ceiling of a nearby church.

For Germans much of the grandeur and significance of Christmas would be lost without a tree. The belief that Luther created the Christmas tree gave it a special religious and cultural meaning.

O Tannenbaum

The glory of the Christmas tree is proclaimed by the German song, *O Tannenbaum,* which is sung to the melody of a student drinking song.[8] Dating from the twelfth century, the melody was popular among the wandering students in France and Germany, often referred to as Goliards and better known for rioting, gambling, and intemperance than scholarship. These medieval vagabonds left behind a treasure trove of poems and songs that remained hidden in a Bavarian monastery for five centuries.

When monasteries were secularized in 1803, their libraries were moved to Munich. Among the contents of the library that came from the village of Benedictbeuern was a manuscript dating from the thirteenth century that had never been cataloged. There were many poems devoted to wine, women, and drink, some of which were passed down through the centuries as student drinking songs and folk songs.[9] One of these student songs is *Lauriger Horatius*, which praises honey-laden wine and ruddy maidens, and has the same melody as *O Tannenbaum. Lauriger Horatius* is also referred to as *Goliardenlied*, a name which underlines its heritage.

Although there is some confusion about dates and facts, August Zarnack is usually credited with setting to music an anonymously written German poem, *O Tannenbaum*, around 1820. Only the first stanza is about fir trees; the other three feature fair maidens, nightingales, and meadow brooks.[10] For the melody Zarnack turned to *Lauriger Horatius*. This melody has attracted other lyrics, one of which is the well-known Civil War song, *Maryland, My Maryland*, written in 1861.

In 1824 Ernest Anschutz, a schoolmaster, kept the first stanza of Zarnack's *O Tannenbaum* and added a second and third stanza. The lyrics followed those of folk songs about the fir tree, one of which is the low German, *O Dannenboom*. Anschutz wanted to give his students a song they could sing about Christmas trees which were growing in popularity in the region and Germany generally. Almost as an oversight, Anschutz made a brief reference in the second stanza to the fir tree as a Christmas tree. In the English version, *O Christmas Tree*, the Christmas tree is extolled in virtually every line.

Christmas in the Bavarian Alps.
Courtesy Inter Nationes

Christmas tree in front of the Cologne Cathedral.
Courtesy Inter Nationes

The Christmas Tree at Windsor Castle

Prince Albert, the German husband of Queen Victoria, played a major role in popularizing the Christmas tree in England. Christmas trees had arrived there earlier, but they did not receive widespread recognition until 1848. That year the *Illustrated London News* showed a drawing of the royal family and featured an article that described the tree:[11]

"The Christmas Tree represented in the Engraving is that which is annually prepared by her Majesty's command for the Royal children. Similar trees are arranged in other apartments of the Castle for her Majesty, his Royal Highness Prince Albert, her Royal Highness the Duchess of Kent, and the Royal household. The tree employed for this festive purpose is

Queen Victoria, Prince Albert, and family around Christmas tree at Windsor Castle in 1848. Courtesy of The Illustrated London News Picture Library

a young fir about eight feet high, and has six tiers of branches. On each tier, or branch, are arranged a dozen wax tapers. Pendent from the branches are elegant trays, baskets, *bonbonnieres*, and other receptacles for sweetmeats, of the most varied and expensive kind; and of all forms, colours, and degrees of beauty. Fancy cakes, gilt gingerbread and eggs filled with sweetmeats, are also suspended by variously-coloured ribbons from the branches. The tree, which stands upon a table covered with white damask, is supported at the root by piles of sweets of a larger kind, and by toys and dolls of all descriptions, suited to the youthful fancy, and to the several ages of the interesting scions of Royalty for whose gratification they are displayed. The name of each recipient is affixed to the doll, bonbon, or other present intended for it, so that no difference of opinion in the choice of dainties may arise to disturb the equanimity of the illustrious juveniles. On the summit of the tree stands the small figure of an angel, with outstretched wings, holding in each hand a wreath. Those trees are objects of much interest to all visitors at the Castle, from Christmas Eve, when they are first set up, until Twelfth Night, when they are finally removed. During this period two trees of similar magnitude and general design stand on the sideboard of the Royal Dining-room, and present a brilliant appearance when all the tapers are lighted up, among the branches. These trees are not accessible to the curiosity of the public; but her Majesty's visitors accompany the Queen from room to room to inspect them when they are illuminated. Her Majesty's tree is furnished by his Royal Highness Prince Albert, whilst that of the Prince is furnished according to the taste of her Majesty. The other trees are jointly provided by her Majesty and the Prince, who plan and arrange the gifts on the table. The trees are constructed and arranged by Mr. Mawditt, the Queen's confectioner."

A Profusion of Christmas Trees in Strasbourg

In 1860, there were stories about the German Christ tree in France and a small fir tree was reportedly sold by a Parisian flower shop that year.[12] Thirty years later, Paris claimed three hundred dealers and shops handling Christmas trees with sales as high as thirty thousand. In spite of this early favorable response, Christmas trees have been less popular in France than Germany and the Scandinavian countries. The exception is Strasbourg and Alsace where a profusion of trees highlights the Christmas holidays. The French have historically given greater emphasis to the New Year's celebration.

Christmas in Denmark

The Lutheran Church gave impetus to the popularity of Christmas trees in the northern countries. Danes enjoy a lavish dinner on Christmas Eve after which someone slips into a nearby room to light the many candles on a decorated tree. Again, a bucket of water is nearby just in case. This precaution is skipped today by those who prefer the less hazardous electric lighting. Everyone anxiously waits and then the door is swung open to show the tree in all its glory, a breathtaking sight every year. For Danish families this moment is the climax of Christmas. Around midnight of New Year's Eve the candles or lights glow for the last time as the New Year is welcomed with traditional songs and toasts.

Christmas Trees with the Flags of Nations

Finnish people like to include rows of flags on their Christmas trees to remind all of friendship among nations. Candles on the tree are lighted for the first time on December 23. At noon on the 24th the "Peace of Christmas" is proclaimed in Turku, the former capital of Finland, a ritual that has been followed for five hundred years. At sunset on Christmas Eve, it is customary for families to place candles on the graves to honor the dead, especially those who have fallen in war. The singing of hymns, including Luther's "A Mighty Fortress," creates a patriotic and religious fervor that is difficult to forget. This tradition can be traced back to pagan days when the winter solstice was a time to placate the ghosts of the dead.

Christmas Trees as Idolatry

The Christmas tree came to Norway by way of Denmark and Germany late in the 19th century. Like the ancient Israelites who were punished by Moses for dancing around a golden calf, many Norwegians initially viewed the Christmas tree as an idolatrous symbol. Soon it became a tradition throughout Norway, first among the more affluent people in such larger cities as Oslo and later in the isolated country towns.

In Belgium, Christmas trees were introduced around 1890 by German businessmen, but they were not widely accepted until the first World War (1914-1918) when people saw the trees of occupying German soldiers.[13] An old Dutch custom is to read the story of the nativity or a folk tale aloud by the flickering Christmas tree lights. Some differences in customs exist in the four linguistic regions of Switzerland; for example, in the French speaking cantons the tree is lit on Christmas Eve but presents are exchanged on New Year's Day.

Irish, Polish, and Czech Trees

Except in such larger cities as Dublin and Wexford, most Irish did not have Christmas trees until recent decades. An important reason was that there were almost no trees in Ireland before the government began a forestation project in 1904. Another was that Christmas trees were seen as a British and Protestant tradition.

Christmas trees first appeared in Poland at the turn of the 18th and 19th century in places then occupied by the Prussians and among burghers of German ancestry.[14] Many decorations on Christmas trees in the Czech Republic are produced by Czech glass blowers who continue to employ a technology that dates back several centuries.

Catholic and Communist Europe

Christmas trees gained a large following in every European country. They became more popular in Protestant northern Europe than in such countries as Italy, Spain, and Portugal with large Catholic populations where the crèche remained as a primary symbol. Climates that are less suitable for the growth of evergreens have also played a role. Christmas trees found their way to Czarist Russia where the Orthodox Church reigned supreme. The Communists, who came into power in 1917, launched a diatribe of anti-religious propaganda and relegated Christmas to a secondary status. They placed the celebration of New Year's Day at center stage and Christmas trees became New Year trees.

Christmas Trees Come to North America

During the early years of the British colonies in North America, Christmas was not generally observed and Christmas trees little known. The exceptions were small communities of German and other European immigrants scattered here and there. All this began to change when German mercenaries arrived to join the British forces in North America in the late 1700's.[15]

Of the 30,000 mercenaries who came to North America, Landgrave Frederick II of Hesse-Cassel supplied 17,000 and Charles I, Duke of Brunswick, provided almost 8,000 with the remainder coming from three other princes.[16] Both Frederick and Charles were related by marriage to the British royal family but the love of money was a more important motive.

A Christmas Gift From the Hessians

Had it not been for a joyous Christmas celebration, the American colonies along with Canada might well have remained a part of the British Empire.

Defeat after defeat had plagued Washington's revolutionary army. Thousands of soldiers had been captured, wounded, or killed, scarce ammunition and supplies were in enemy hands, and the enlistments of most soldiers were soon to expire. After the army of British commander Sir William Howe pushed the rebel forces through New Jersey across the Delaware river into Pennsylvania, something had to be done if the revolutionary cause was to survive. Washington decided to attack the enemy garrison of Hessians in Trenton.

The Hessians were a formidable fighting force that had proven military prowess in previous battles.[17] Washington knew that he couldn't defeat them on their terms. Why not recross the ice-strewn Delaware river and march to Trenton in the dark of night for a surprise attack!

Howe was more interested in his mistress, a wife of one of his officers, than pursuing Washington's defeated army. Colonel Johann Gottlieb Rahl, Hessian commander in Trenton, was more interested in celebrating Christmas.[18] Though he was informed about a possible attack, Rahl felt little threat from Washington's ragged army. Duty hours were reduced to a minimum and adequate defensive measures ignored.

Christmas Eve was a special time for the Hessians, a time to drink heartily, sing the old songs, and talk of the homeland. So they did on that evening of December 24, 1776 in the houses, churches, and barracks in which they were quartered. A ration of rum helped overcome uncomfortable quarters and the bitterly cold weather on the outside.[19] There were regimental musicians to play the familiar melodies and lead in the singing. Thoughts turned to Christmas in Hesse-Cassel and the beautiful candle-lit Christmas trees.

A small group of Americans of uncertain origin did attack on the evening of Christmas Day but were easily repulsed.[20] Rahl was convinced that there was little else the Americans could do and felt sufficiently secure to further reduce duty rosters. The Hessians returned to a hearty celebration of Christmas.[21] Early in the morning of December 26, Washington's forces attacked.

Showered by sleet and snow the ragged Americans suddenly appeared everywhere, or so it seemed to the hapless Hessians. They fired from behind trees and houses, and their cannons created havoc in the icy streets. The Hessians attempted to form ranks to defend their positions and counterattack the enemy. Awakened in his headquarters, Rahl was groggy from a night of drink and celebration.[22] He valiantly tried to rally his forces until late in the battle when he was struck by two musket balls and fell from his horse, mortally wounded. As he was carried from the field,

Old Barracks at Trenton. During the Revolutionary War, the Barracks were filled with captured British prisoners of war and later with Colonial troops. When the Barracks fell into British hands, it became quarters for the Hessian mercenaries, most of whom were taken prisoner by Washington in the Battle of Trenton. Courtesy Library of Congress

Hessian morale collapsed and the battle was lost. British and Hessian troops of cavalry might have turned the tide but their only concern was to ride out of Trenton as quickly as possible. Washington did not lose a single man in the fight. Five Hessian officers including Rahl died, 101 men were killed or wounded, and 868 were captured.

Hessian Christmas Trees

A few evergreen trees from the surrounding New Jersey forests were undoubtedly a part of the well-planned Hessian Christmas festivities. The trees would have been roughly hewed and simply decorated, not likely to attract eyewitnesses. Washington had higher priorities than to receive reports on Hessian Christmas trees. Many of the ragged colonial troops came from communities that gave little attention to Christmas and were not familiar with Christmas trees. They wouldn't know one if they saw one.

The Hessians played an important role in bringing Christmas trees to America. During their wartime Christmas celebrations many of them cut and decorated a Christmas tree, especially for families in homes where they were billeted. They were said to have set up candle-lit Christmas trees for the children of Newport, Rhode Island. More than one third, including many of those captured in Trenton, remained in the United States by deserting or escaping as prisoners of war. Christmas festivities in their new American homes would surely have included a Christmas tree. In 1804, a captain decorated a Christmas tree at Fort Dearborn, Michigan, a custom he claimed to have learned from the Hessians.

Christmas Tree in Blue Room, St. George Tucker House. Photograph by Jane Smith, courtesy of the Colonial Williamsburg Foundation

A Hessian Christmas Tree in Washington's Williamsburg

Charles Minnigerode from Hesse-Darmstadt arrived in 1842 to teach Greek and Latin at the College of William and Mary in Washington's favorite city, Williamsburg, Virginia. He became a close friend of Judge Nathaniel Beverley Tucker, a fellow professor, and almost a part of the Tucker family.[23] The children called him Minck and were delighted with the tales that he told about his childhood. They were given a special treat by their newly-found friend that Christmas. Minnigerode and Beverley, as the Judge was called, strolled into the woods, cut a small evergreen and placed it on a parlor table. The tree was decorated with homemade ornaments, candles wired to the branches, and a gold star on the top.

St. George Tucker House. Photograph by Tom Green, courtesy Colonial Williamsburg Foundation

The Tucker house is one of the oldest in Colonial Williamsburg and dates back some three hundred years.[24] St. George Tucker, the father of Beverley, became the owner in 1788 and immediately moved the house a hundred and twenty feet around the corner to face a more prestigious street. Rooms, roofs, chimneys, stairways, windows, and basements were added, deleted, and changed to accommodate the needs of family and lifestyle. A first for the time was a chamberpot cubicle next to Tucker's bedroom. As an accomplished horticulturist, Tucker planted an orchard, a vegetable garden, and a pleasure garden. In earlier days eleven slaves were quartered out back.

In 1929, the house was deeded to Colonial Williamsburg with rent-free use by the occupants for life. The last of five generations of the Tucker family to live there died in 1992 after which the house was

Christmas tree at Ellis Island, 1905. Ellis Island was the major point of entry for German and other immigrants from 1892 to 1943 taking the place of Castle Garden opened in 1855 on the southern tip of Manhattan. Boston and New Orleans were also important ports of entry. Courtesy State Historical Society of Wisconsin and Ellis Island Immigration Museum

repaired, repainted, and refurnished. During each of the three Christmases the house was closed, an admirer left a small tree on the porch. In 1996, the newly opened St. George Tucker House celebrated Christmas with a tree on a table in the Blue Room and a ceiling-high tree in the family room. The ornaments were hand made and there were candles.

The First Christmas Tree in Canada

In addition to the Hessians, other German mercenaries who came to fight for the British were familiar with Christmas trees. The Brunswick contingent fought in major campaigns in Canada and the Colonies. Their commander Major General Friedreich Adolph von Riedesel is given credit for introducing the Christmas tree in Canada.[25]

In 1781, General von Riedesel became the commander of all British troops from Montreal north to the city of Sorel. A few days before Christmas von Riedesel and his family moved into their Sorel home, the site of central military headquarters. British officers and neighbors invited to their Christmas party were astonished to see for the first time a Christmas tree decorated and illuminated in the German tradition.

During early years, most Canadians followed English customs and celebrated Christmas with holly and mistletoe but without trees. Within a short time however, immigrants from Germany and other European countries made Christmas trees traditional in every part of Canada.

German Immigrants and Their Christmas Trees

A few Germans came to America in 1608 with the English Captain John Smith, who founded Jamestown, Virginia.[26] Small groups seeking religious and political freedom followed during the next few decades. In 1683, thirteen Quaker families from Krefeld arrived in Pennsylvania and established Germantown on the outskirts of Philadelphia.[27] By the time of the first American census in 1790, the number of Germans in Pennsylvania totaled 225,000 or one-third of the state population. From 1820 to the present more than seven million Germans had immigrated and today a quarter of Americans claim a German heritage.

The Germans changed America as much as it changed them. Their customs and traditions became a part of the American mainstream, but not without playing havoc with what had gone before. Ignoring the prohibitions of Puritanism, the Germans guzzled huge quantities of beer even on the Sabbath. They celebrated Christmas which had been banned in early New England and frowned upon for many years.

An American Tradition

The joy of Christmas for German immigrants began with a Christmas tree with decorations and lit-candles. For the children there were toys from the local store and sometimes from grandparents in Germany. All joined to sing Christmas carols they learned as children. Much talk of the homeland, a little marzipan and candy, and a few drinks to wet the vocal cords and ease the pain of homesickness.

The Christmas trees of millions of German immigrants became millions more as their neighbors witnessed them. Other European immigrants, especially those from Scandinavia, had become equally fond of the Christmas tree in their countries. A German and European tradition soon became an American tradition.

Willa Cather's Christmas Tree

American novelist, Willa Cather, was nine years old in 1885 when she moved from Virginia to frontier Nebraska. The modest house in Red Cloud where she lived with her parents and six brothers and sisters has been preserved as though she never left it. After graduating from the University of Nebraska in 1895, Cather spent most of her adult life in New York City and returned only for brief visits to Red Cloud. Yet, she never lost her attachment to the Nebraska of her youth. In her words, she "knew every farm, every tree, every field in the region around my home and they all called out to me."

The Austrians, Bohemians, Swedes, Germans, Russians, and Norwegians in the novel, *My Ántonia,* were like the real ones who came to the Nebraska frontier. Willa Cather understood the problems created by the language barriers, the cultural and social differences, the trauma of homesickness, and the hardships of frontier life. With simplicity and sensitivity, Cather described this mixture of diversity and how it was gradually being blended to create the Americans who reside in Red Cloud today.

The Christmas tree that stands each year in Willa Cather's house reaches back to the frontier days of her youth. In *My Ántonia,* Cather wrote about that time in the words of Jim Burden, the narrator in her novel:

"On the day before Christmas, Jake packed the things we were sending to the Shimerdas in his saddle-bags and set off on grandfather's grey gelding. When he mounted his horse at the door, I saw that he had a hatchet slung to his belt, and he gave grandmother a meaning look which told me he was planning a surprise for me. That afternoon I watched long and eagerly from the sitting-room window. At last I saw a dark spot moving on the west hill, beside the half-buried cornfield, where the sky was taking on a coppery flush from the sun that did note quite break through. I put on my cap and ran out to meet Jake. When I got to the pond, I could see that he was bringing in a little cedar tree across his pommel. He used to help my father cut Christmas trees for me in Virginia, and he had not forgotten how much I like them.

By the time we had placed the cold, fresh-smelling little tree in a corner of the sitting-room, it was already Christmas Eve. After supper we all gathered there, and even grandfather, reading his paper by the

Childhood home of Willa Cather in Red Cloud, Nebraska. Photograph by Patricia K. Phillips

13

Christmas tree at the Willa Cather house decorated with stringed popcorn and candles.
Photograph by Patricia K. Phillips

Austria. There was a bleeding heart, in tufts of paper lace; there were the three kings, gorgeously apparelled, and the ox and the ass and the shepherds; there was the Baby in the manger, and a group of angels, singing; there were camels and leopards, held by the black slaves of the three kings. Our tree became the talking tree of the fairy tale; legends and stories nestled like birds in its branches. Grandmother said it reminded her of the Tree of Knowledge. We put sheets of cotton wool under it for a snow-field, and Jake's pocket-mirror for a frozen lake."[28]

The Bible and a Christmas Tree in a Log Cabin

In the 1850's, Erick and Anna Selland emigrated to America from Norway with their two small children, son, Erick, and daughter, Eli. After settling for a year in Wisconsin, the Selland family set out with a covered wagon to homestead in northern Iowa near the town of Decorah.[29] Travel was extremely slow. The wagon was a heavy load for two horses, and the two cows tied to the rear had to be rested at frequent intervals. In the wagon were the Selland's household belongings and a big chest packed with valuables. The children sometimes sat on the top of the chest as the miles slowly passed.

Each parent took a turn driving the team of horses with the other prodding the two cows. One day Anna was in the driver's seat as Erick walked behind. All

table, looked up with friendly interest now and then. The cedar was about five feet high and very shapely. We hung it with the gingerbread animals, strings of popcorn, and bits of candle which Fuchs had fitted into pasteboard sockets. Its real splendours, however, came from the most unlikely place in the world — from Otto's cowboy trunk. I had never seen anything in that trunk but old boots and spurs and pistols, and a fascinating mixture of yellow leather thongs, cartridges. and shoemaker's wax. From under the lining he now produced a collection of brilliantly coloured paper fixtures, several inches high and stiff enough to stand alone. They had been sent to him year after year, by his old mother in

The log cabin built by Erick Selland in 1853 was dismantled, stored, and reassembled for display in Vesterheim Museum. Photograph by Darrell D. Henning, courtesy Vesterheim Museum

was quiet except for the sounds of the wagon wheels and animal footsteps. Suddenly there was a loud and plaintive cry from Erick. Anna found her husband down on his knees sobbing, "Oh, Erick, Erick!"

Their son, Erick, had fallen off the big chest and the heavy wheel of the covered wagon had crushed his body and taken his life. The loss was almost too much to bear. Into a deep hole dug by his father, the grieving parents lowered little Erick. They lingered awhile at his grave in the prairie and then moved on toward the new homestead.

Every year a Christmas tree is displayed in the Selland log cabin. Photograph by Darrell D. Henning, courtesy Vesterheim Museum

Their first home was a crude one-room cabin built with round logs sealed with clay. Erick envisioned a new cabin when he found a huge virgin pine tree, five feet in diameter. The tree was felled, logs cut, and then Erick and a neighbor began to saw the logs into slabs. A big hole was dug under each log. One man stood in the hole and the other on the log drawing the saw back and forth. The work began in the summer continued through the fall and into winter when Erick began hauling the slabs home. The cabin started taking shape in the spring but there was hard work for another two years. Finally, Erick could admire his new cabin with one main room, fourteen feet wide and sixteen feet long, and an upstairs room. All built from one giant pine tree.

The house originally built about 1853 was dismantled by Selland descendants around 1908 and the slabs stored. Later the slabs were donated to the Vesterheim Museum in Decorah, Iowa, and in 1933 the first floor of the cabin was reconstructed within the museum. In the cabin are reminders of the pioneer family that made it home. Along one wall is the iron range upon which Anna Selland cooked meals for family and friends as well as relatives from Norway who stayed for a time. A spinning wheel, a cradle, and a rocking chair define Anna's life in other ways. The large family Bible, well worn with use, dates from the days when religious services were held in the house. Chapter two of the Gospel of St. Luke expressed the meaning of Christmas as the family and friends gathered for food and joy. The Bible and the Christmas tree recreate the fellowship and spirit of that time.

A Christmas Tree Industry

The immigrants and their descendants created a demand for Christmas trees that could only be supplied by the vast untapped American forests. Even in rural areas the fir trees on the family farm or a nearby timber were soon too few. It became necessary to import trees for sale in local stores from more distant forests. In the cities there was an even greater demand for Christmas trees. American entrepreneurship and ingenuity soon filled the gap that marked the beginnings of a Christmas tree industry. The pioneers who solved the problem of supplying millions of Christmas trees every year encountered a myriad of challenges.

A FOCUS ON THE PIONEERS

Christmas Tree Markets

Many early American immigrants cut their own Christmas trees from local timbers or nearby forests. For small communities, dry goods and grocery stores brought trees from the countryside or bought them from a fledgling entrepreneur. As demand grew in larger urban centers, sizable markets for trees began to appear. One of the earliest had its beginning in 1851 when Yankee ingenuity and German immigration combined to create the first Christmas tree market in New York City.[1]

Mark Carr Makes Some Easy Money

Mark Carr lived in the Catskill Mountains where fir and spruce trees were free for the cutting. With only the cost of transportation to consider, Carr thought that he could make a little money. In spite of skeptical comments from Carr's wife, Carr and sons loaded two ox carts full of trees and hauled them to the nearest ship landing for transport to New York City.

Carr rented space for one silver dollar in Washington Market, a large produce market, and almost immediately the trees were sold. He couldn't believe how easy it had all been. After a few days in New York to enjoy their good fortune, Carr and the boys returned home to gloat about it. The following year they sold more trees and continued to do so for many years. A member of the Carr family was still hauling trees to New York in 1898.

The Carrs immediately faced competition as their Catskill neighbors envied the easy money. Soon the small space Carr leased for a dollar expanded into a large Christmas tree market. Space eventually became so scarce and expensive that some dealers began to sell trees directly off the ships. Small trees sold for five to ten cents, larger eight to ten foot trees for a quarter. More costly were trees twenty feet or taller, a few reached above the masts of the ships in which they arrived. Prime customers for tall trees were German Sunday schools and the saloons in which Germans drank beer.

Trees From More Distant Places

In a few years Carr and his neighbors faced a scarcity of trees as cutting far exceeded the growth potential of wild Catskill trees. They could supply only a small fraction of an ever increasing demand. Trees began to come to New York from such distant places as New Hampshire and Massachusetts. By the 1880's more than two hundred thousand trees came into the Washington Market by wagons, trains, and ships.[2]

The trees were bundled like cordwood twice the height of a man or stood on their cut ends in long rows. They reached several blocks inland from the waterfront. It became difficult to walk on the sidewalks with mountains of trees on each side keeping out the sunlight. Nearby shopkeepers had to use gas lights even at noon.

Harvesting wild trees for an early Christmas tree market.

New Markets for Trees

Large tree markets began to appear elsewhere. In New England where the celebration of Christmas had long been shunned, Boston became a major trading center for Christmas trees. By 1900, more than a million trees a year were shipped from Maine to Boston and New York. The forests in Virginia and Maryland provided the trees for Washington, D.C. Later Los Angeles became an important distribution point for the west coast. Trees for the large German population in Chicago came from Michigan, a sizable number in the Christmas tree ship of August and Herman Schuenemann.[3]

The Schuenemann Christmas Tree Ship

Every year beginning as early as 1887, the Schuenemann brothers cut trees in Michigan, loaded them on a fishing schooner, and sailed across Lake Michigan to Chicago. People anxiously awaited the annual arrival at the Clark Street bridge to buy a tree at a modest price. In 1898 the ship did not arrive. August Schuenemann had set sail and when a storm arose he and the ship were lost. His younger brother, Herman, decided to carry on alone and for eleven years many people depended on him for their trees. In 1912 tragedy struck again as the gales of Lake Michigan took the life of Herman and his crew of seventeen. Later, on December 5 off the coast of Wisconsin, a fisherman found the tops of spruce trees entangled in his nets. A few days later a bottle with a farewell message written on a page of the ship's log by the captain was recovered.

The next year, 1913, the Christmas ship again appeared at the Clark Street dock. There on deck was Herman's wife who had hired wood-cutters to help with the trees. For twenty-two years her ship arrived to deliver trees for a merrier Christmas. In 1924, Herman Schuenemann's fully intact wallet was found where the spruce trees had entangled the nets twelve years earlier. Three years after that another bottle with a farewell note from a crew member was retrieved.

Pioneers Who Built an Industry

John H. Hofert: Pioneer and Entrepreneur

John H. Hofert bred and trained draft horses for work on his farm along the Mississippi River near St. Paul, Minnesota. To supplement family income, his teams and wagons hauled cargo for the Great Northern Railroad. In 1880, always on the lookout for new opportunities, Hofert began to cut Christmas trees in forests near Moose Lake, Minnesota, and used his wagons to haul them to Minneapolis for sale. Profits were excellent and within ten years the business had expanded to Chicago and beyond.

John H. Hofert, 1855-1934, founder of the J. Hofert Company.

In 1902, Hofert abandoned the cold winters of the Middle West for sunny California. The climate of Los Angeles pleased him and his wife whose health problems had prompted the move. Hofert missed the business he had left behind in Minnesota. He began cutting wild trees in the forests of California and Oregon and expanded as the railroads built track up and down the coast from San Diego to Seattle.

Business acumen helped the Hoferts survive the Great Depression of the thirties. John Hofert and son, Alvin, would see a fine crop of Christmas trees and ask the farmer what he wanted for them. Many farmers would give the trees to the Hoferts for a bottle of whisky or nothing at all because they wanted the land cleared for planting. During the years that followed, the Hoferts built one of the largest Christmas tree enterprises in North America.

G. R. Kirk Came for Gold in Alaska

Attracted by the gold rush in Alaska, George Ridgway Kirk, known as G. R., left his home in Pennsylvania for Seattle in 1898, and almost immediately sailed north to make his fortune. Misfortune met him instead. G. R. found miners digging holes for the victims of an epidemic rather than the gold that had lured him there.

G. R. returned to Pennsylvania and then spent a few years in North Carolina to learn the lumber business. He was back in the northwest by 1902 and made it his home and place of business. A disastrous fire in his highly successful planing mill and the competitive impact of steel posts on a wooden post venture

George Ridgway Kirk, known as G.R., founder of the Kirk Company.

caused some difficult times. Then in 1918 a brother-in-law in El Paso, Texas, called G. R. to tell him "that a florist down here wants a carload of Christmas trees." A stupid idea, thought G. R., as he told his foreman to cut this Texan a carload of wild Douglas fir trees. The next year came an order for two more carloads. That got G. R.'s attention. He immediately cut three carloads for himself and headed for Los Angeles where he set up shop at the 8th and Alameda railroad tracks. He sold all of his trees and each year

thereafter came back with a few more carloads. This marked the beginning of decades of competition with the J. Hofert Company.

Selling Christmas Trees in a General Store

During the early 1900's, Charles H. Strathmeyer owned a store in York, Pennsylvania, where he sold dry goods, groceries, and notions. With a large German population dating back to colonial days, Christmas trees had always been popular in Pennsylvania. At the turn of the century, the demand for trees increased rapidly. A good supply of wild red cedar and jack pine trees was available in the timbers of the surrounding countryside. Why not cut and haul them to the store and make a little extra profit? Son Charles, Jr. could provide low cost labor. Years later Charles, Jr. commented that "you had to walk and drag a great deal to get enough trees."

Strathmeyer general store during the early 1900's. Christmas trees were sold on the porch.

G. R. Kirk tagging trees in the early days of his Christmas tree business.

Loading truck for transport to the rail yards for shipment.

Andrew and Margaret Abraczinskas.

An Immigrant From Lithuania Makes His Mark

In the 1890's Andrew Abraczinskas immigrated to the United States from Lithuania with his parents, four brothers, and a sister. The family settled in Shenandoah, Pennsylvania, where the father started a grocery store. When they arrived none of them could speak, read, or write the English language.

Andrew worked in the anthracite coal mines, helped in his father's store, and at age twenty-three married Margaret Ginnis. Seven years later Andrew and Margaret bought a farm and moved fifteen miles and two mountains away from the coal mines. Andrew sawed the plentiful supply of timber into lumber to enlarge the house for his family of four sons and a daughter. Cows provided milk and the land produced an abundance of potatoes, fruit, and nuts. A wonderful home for a growing family.

An avid reader of the agricultural bulletins, Andrew once grafted an apple tree to grow five different species of fruit. He liked to experiment and was always ready to buy more land.

Andrew made a good income from lumber and continually planted trees to provide for the future. Seedlings were grown in every nook and cranny of the farm and then replanted to replace the cut trees. Eventually several acres were devoted to growing Norway spruce and pine transplants which marked the beginning of the Abraczinskas Christmas tree business.

In the twenties Andrew developed a technique for shearing Scotch pine that attracted the attention of universities and Christmas tree growers in several states. Andrew was ahead of the times. Today, most of the millions of Christmas trees grown in North America are sheared. More about shearing later. Andrew died in 1956 and his wife, Margaret, in 1961.

The Kirk Company

G. R. Kirk, who was introduced earlier, shipped three carloads of Christmas trees to Los Angeles in 1919. Large annual increases followed. By 1928, the Kirk Company was producing twenty to twenty-five carloads, each of which carried about a thousand trees. That year brought an end to the prosperity of the twenties. The stock market crash in October of 1929 marked the beginning of the longest and worst economic depression in American history.

The depression made it difficult to make ends meet. Through ingenuity and extra effort, G. R. Kirk met the challenge and set the stage for future growth. At this time G. R.'s son, Paul, did not yet know the important role he was to play in the company.

Paul Kirk in his 1924 Model T Roadster which he took on the road to sell Christmas trees throughout the United States.

In 1928, Paul Kirk was a junior at the University of Washington, and like so many Americans, witnessed the hectic speculation in a booming stock market. Fortunes were made almost overnight as the market rose to new heights. A career as a stock-broker had exciting prospects for Paul, even more than his father's Christmas tree business.

Paul decided to stay out of college to earn money to pay for his senior year. Although he had strong feelings that a son should not work for his father, Paul agreed to become employed in the company on a temporary basis. The fall was spent harvesting trees at Shelton, Washington, which involved some hard physical labor. Later Paul followed the trees to Los Angeles to sell them at the railway "team tracks."

The Kirk family in later years. Paul Ridgway Kirk, Sr., sitting, Morris L. "Mac" Kirk, left, Paul R. "Rick" Kirk Jr., who is now the company president, center, and Ann Kirk Davis, right.

Paul returned for his senior year, graduated, and began working for a brokerage. By this time the stock market had crashed and the euphoria of the boom had ended. The depression became ever more critical as millions of people lost their jobs. Among them was Paul who returned home in 1931 and agreed to work for his father but on temporary basis. G. R. had made an offer that was difficult to refuse. "I'll tell you what I will do," G. R. said. "You have no job. I'll give you a 1924 Model T Ford roadster. Why don't you go into Colorado, Texas and Oklahoma and come back through Kansas City and see what kind of tree market is down there."

The last of the three Kirk house trailers. From left to right, Ann Kirk, Paul Ridgway Kirk, Sr., and Paul "Rick" Kirk, Jr.

At the depth of the depression, Paul married an attractive young lady, Dorothy Fisher. With a sense of adventure, the newlyweds decided to follow-up on Paul's earlier travels to gain more insights on marketing Christmas trees. Money was scarce and house trailers were not available in the Northwest, so they built a fifteen-foot house trailer from scratch. There was barely enough space for the studio couch, an icebox and gasoline stove, a cupboard, and clothing. The next ten years Paul and Dorothy spent much of their time in this and two other trailers traveling throughout the United States and Canada. They not only expanded the market for Kirk trees but made hundreds of friends during their visits. As Paul Kirk later recalled, "We visited people everywhere and they visited us. We would park our trailer in back yards, had produce customers that handled our trees come in for breakfast and then later return loaded down with oranges and apples for us. We had nothing but fun in those days." The friendships that resulted became important in buying Kirk trees. During this time Paul and Dorothy became the proud parents of three children, all of whom joined the travels and the fun.

The Kirks expanded sales that in turn required more trees. Most were delivered to small grocery stores on consignment. Gradually chain stores began to take greater numbers of Kirk trees.

The Hoferts and the Kirks

The J. Hofert Company roamed in the same forests and markets as the Kirk Company, and competition reigned supreme. Throughout the years that followed it became increasingly difficult for the Hoferts to retain a competitive advantage. Paul Kirk's dynamic personality and drive challenged the Hoferts at every turn.

The Kirk Company in the early thirties began to produce large numbers of Douglas firs in Montana that helped capture markets in the Midwest. These trees could withstand cold conditions better than those from Washington. To get more of the Montana-type trees for an expanding market, the Kirks began to harvest trees in British Columbia not far from Lake Louise and Banff. At one time a half million trees were shipped from this area.

In 1936, during his travels in the Maritime Provinces of Canada, Paul found a large supply of spruce and Balsam firs for the huge Northeastern market. He moved quickly and set up 50 centers in Nova Scotia, New Brunswick, and Quebec to which farmers brought wild trees to be graded and tied. During one year the Kirk Company reached a peak of 400 carloads. The J. Hofert Company was also competing in that market which was so large that both companies could prosper but neither wanted to give the other any advantage.

Minnesota Table Top Trees

The Kirks developed a major venture in Minnesota by cutting table top trees out of black spruce. As Paul explained, "The trees were small, grew in swamps and had no timber value. But they had a beautiful little tree in their top three feet." The trees were cut, put on wooden stands, and painted silver or green. As many as 250 thousand trees were shipped in one year, primarily to large chain stores. In the sixties and seventies artificial trees from Hong Kong destroyed this profitable business.

The Industry Pioneers in Perspective

From the days of Mark Carr to the turn of the century, hundreds of other entrepreneurs were cutting trees in forests and timbers to meet the demand for Christmas trees. Their names cannot be found on the pages of history but they made a major contribution nonetheless. Few of their businesses have survived. The Hoferts, the Kirks, the Strathmeyers, and the Abraczinskas were not only early pioneers but played a major role in developing the Christmas tree industry. In the beginning they cut wild trees with little regard for replanting and conservation. Later they began to cultivate and shape the trees in the forests and then grow millions of trees on plantations.

An early Kirk Company mechanized Christmas tree yard, the basis for large scale harvesting and shipping.

Christmas Trees are Banned

Saving the Forests for the Trees

Forests have the capacity to replenish themselves if seed trees are left standing, but could not withstand the high rate of cutting that took place. The demand for Christmas trees grew so rapidly that by the beginning of the twentieth century one in five Americans had a tree. An even heavier toll was taken by the cutting of trees for fuel, lumber, and paper. One-half of the original timber stand in the United States was depleted. Many people saw a need for conservation but not everyone agreed. Then came a president of the United States who had no doubts about the matter.

A Christmas Tree in a White House Closet

Upon becoming president after the assassination of McKinley in 1901, Theodore Roosevelt used the White House as a bully pulpit to damn the "malefactors of great wealth." Among other things he thought that the American forests had been stripped bare and wasted through the quest for profits. Christmas trees were not spared and to make his point, Roosevelt banned them in the White House.

Roosevelt's sons, Archie and Quentin, thought otherwise and surprised their father with a Christmas tree they had hidden in a closet. For punishment Roosevelt sent them to fellow-conservationist Gifford Pinchot for a lecture. Pinchot gave Christmas trees and the boys a boost by telling the President that the problem could be solved through proper forest management. Wonderful news for the two ingenuous boys!

There was no need to ban Christmas trees or restrict their number. The thinning that occurred could benefit the forest. By the early 1950's more than thirty million Christmas trees were grown in the United States and Canada.

President Theodore Roosevelt who banned Christmas trees in the White House. Photographic Collection, State Historical Society of Iowa

Quentin and Archie who challenged the Christmas tree ban by hiding a tree in a White House closet. Courtesy Library of Congress

Christmas Tree Plantations

Companies like J. Hofert and Kirk had the resources that enabled them to move rapidly into new potentially profitable ventures and out of those that were not. For example, in 1950 Paul Kirk decided to produce Scotch pine trees in Canada east of Toronto and in a few years nearly a thousand acres were planted. Many of these trees were sheared which involves cutting back the soft new foliar growth to give them a better shape. If you could shear Scotch pine trees, thought Paul Kirk, why not shear Douglas fir and other wild trees! He didn't want competitors to know, so he began by shearing ten acres in secret. Eventually the Kirks sheared two thousand acres of wild trees in Canada and Washington, but it was difficult to maintain good quality.

The Kirks, the Hoferts, and others began to see that naturally reseeded wild trees, even when fertilized and sheared, did not provide the best solution for supplying Christmas trees.

The Seeds of Change

Until the early forties, most Christmas trees were cut from naturally reseeded forests or from abandoned farms and pastures and then transported by rail and water to the market. Some of this cutting violated good conservation practices, but as Gifford Pinchot pointed out to President Theodore Roosevelt, Christmas trees were not the primary culprits. Through systematic cutting a continuous supply of trees become available. The cutting can be beneficial which is the reason lumber companies contracted with the Kirks and Hoferts to thin out their timber forests. The major change that began to occur after World War II came as much for economic reasons as the need for conservation.

The First Christmas Tree Farm

W. V. McGalliard became a harbinger of the future when he established the first Christmas tree farm in New Jersey. Today, more than 90 percent of Christmas trees are grown in this way. The son of McGalliard reported that in the spring of 1901 his father planted some twenty-five thousand Norway spruce on their farm in Mercer County about four or five miles from Trenton.[4] The trees came from Charles Black who owned a nursery in Hightstown, New Jersey, and were probably imported from the Scandinavian countries. Twenty thousand of them were eight to fourteen inch transplants and five thousand were seedlings. It was the son's recollection that all came packed in moss in large wooden piano shipping cases. They were planted four feet apart and cultivated as long as feasible.

The reasons McGalliard decided to go into Christmas tree farming are interesting. The farm had a ten acre gravelly field on which it had become impossible to grow a profitable farm crop. McGalliard noticed that the Norway spruce hedge along the road at the front of his farm grew well on poor soil. Putting two and two together, he figured that Christmas trees might be a good gamble on the ten-acre field. An excellent market in nearby Trenton was a positive factor.

When the trees were ready for market in 1907 or 1908, as the son recalled, a flat price of one dollar each was established. Some customers selected a tree in the field and it would be cut for them to take home. A sizable number tagged their trees weeks in advance for delivery at Christmas. Fifty or more trees were loaded on a farm wagon drawn by a team of horses and hauled to Trenton. The price of one dollar was maintained for many years. After the original crop was harvested, several other plantings of Norway spruce were made by McGalliard and later by a son.

Pioneering is a Slow Process

McGalliard's pioneering venture had little immediate impact on the industry. Eighteen years later, Murray Stewart planted two and one-half acres of white and American red pine seedlings to grow Christmas trees on a steep hillside in Center Township, Pennsylvania. A few others followed with tree plantations, but as Stewart pointed out, "Pioneering in any line is usually a slow process and Christmas tree farming was no exception."[5] It was not until the thirties and forties that the idea really grew.

Musser Forests, Inc., Indiana, Pennsylvania

At a time when most Christmas trees were spruce and fir, Fred Musser of Indiana, Pennsylvania, decided that good color and needle retention of pines would more than offset the greater difficulty of decorating a long-needled tree.[6] In 1928, Musser planted six hundred thousand pine and spruce seedlings on four hundred acres of farmland. Some of these trees were to be sold as Christmas trees in five or six years and the remainder left to become larger growth timber. Musser had visions of great wealth as he checked and re-checked his figures.

Fred Musser, Sr. in the 1940's, founder of Musser Forests, Inc.

Musser decided to test the market with pine trees already growing on various tracts of farm land including coal company property reforested by his father. He cut eleven carloads of trees and shipped them to Buffalo on consignment.[7] With his estimate of a thousand dollars for each carload, the trees would give him enough money to pay all of his debts and then some or so he thought. Actual receipts totaled $198 for the eleven carloads.

Musser was an excellent salesman who had won a national dealer prize for selling Chryslers and an optimist by nature. In spite of the first dismal results, Musser continued to ship pines on consignment. The Red pine was one of his favorites but the Scotch pine was always at the top of the list. Through his personal sales efforts and extensive radio and newspaper advertising, Musser rapidly expanded the market for Scotch pines. By 1970, the Scotch pine had overtaken the lead of the Douglas fir as the most popular Christmas tree in America.

The quality of the seed became a major factor in the competitive race to grow Scotch pine trees. Always ahead of the game, Musser decided to raise seedlings for his own use and, since he couldn't keep other growers out of the market, why not sell his quality seedlings to them. In 1938, a nursery operation was begun with sixty seed beds, ten employees, and a single price sheet for growers.

The growth of Musser Forests, Inc. has been phenomenal! What began with evergreen seedlings has expanded to a full line of trees and other plantings. Today there are three thousand nursery beds, each 100 by 4 feet in size, producing more than thirty-five million seedlings, transplants and rooted cuttings each year. Much of the operation was automated with the most efficient machinery and equipment available. There are refrigerated storage buildings, greenhouses, a retail garden center, and an elaborate irrigation system for which water is supplied by a thirty acre manmade lake. What began as a single price sheet has become a forty page, four color order catalog mailed to more than one-half million people.

In addition to the two thousand acres of nurseries, a Christmas tree plantation of more than six thousand acres is annually increased in size. Some of the trees are grown to provide timber as Fred Musser originally planned. From a hundred to three hundred people are employed on a seasonal basis and shipments are made to every part of North America.

Fred Musser Sr., who died in 1988, must truly be called an industry pioneer. He was not only the leading advocate of the Scotch pine but provided for himself and other growers the nursery stock to improve the quality of Christmas trees. The diversity and scale of Musser Forests, Inc. attest to his energy and entrepreneurial skills. Finally, he assured it's survival through his son, Fred Musser, Jr., the present president, and daughter, Nancy Musser, vice president, who plays a major role in advertising and marketing.

Strathmeyer Forests

Charles W. Strathmeyer began his sojourn with Christmas trees when he "had to walk and drag to get enough trees" for his father's grocery store early in the century. In spite of this hard work, Charles thought that selling trees was a good idea. They did make a profit, at least some of the time. But there must be a better way to get trees! So in 1932, Charles planted seedlings in nurseries for future Christmas tree harvests. Today, Strathmeyer Forests, Inc. grows trees on more than a thousand acres in south central Pennsylvania.

Like Fred Musser, Fred Strathmeyer, the son of Charles W., diversified into the nursery business, "I'm in two seasonal businesses—the nursery business in the spring and the Christmas trees in winter." Strathmeyer sells between three and four million seedlings every spring which is the largest part of his business.

As Strathmeyer expressed it, Christmas trees are sold "any way we can." Strathmeyer has wholesale and retail customers, sells through service clubs, in parking lots, straight off the farm, and by mail. As many as eight service clubs, such as Sertoma and the Lions, have played a major role in boosting tree sales. Customers can also choose and cut their trees, an idea that Strathmeyer says has "taken off nationwide like gangbusters. You're not just selling the tree, but the experience. Families with children especially like it."

A Strathmeyer product with an environmental theme is the individually-packaged evergreen seedlings that come in recyclable bags and planting instructions. Hundreds of thousands of these packets are sold, a good way to increase income during off-season. Grocery chains and other companies have given away thousands of seedlings to their customers, stockholders and employees to show their concern for the environment. Guests at weddings and anniversary parties receive the seedlings as environmentally-friendly favors.

Strathmeyer continues to develop superior seed by digging up the best trees and replanting them in an orchard. Since trees take 20 to 40 years to develop seed, Strathmeyer says, "I won't see it, but at least the kids will." His children, Brian, Gerrit, Tim, Fred, and Robin all work in the business.

Franklin D. Roosevelt, Christmas Tree Farmer

President Franklin D. Roosevelt was as interested in conservation as his distant cousin President Theodore Roosevelt.[8] Throughout his life, F.D.R. was not only a strong advocate of conservation but practiced conservation on his estate in Hyde Park, New York, and proved that it can pay. He first learned that forestry can reap rewards during a visit to Germany in 1891 where, for a time, he attended a *Volkschule* in Bad Nauheim. On a bicycle trip that summer, Franklin came to a town near a great forest. As he said in a speech fifty years later, "For over two hundred years that town in

Germany had to pay no taxes . . . it was a forest on an annual yield basis . . . every year they planted new trees. And every year the proceeds from that forest paid the equivalent of taxes."[9]

While still a young man, Franklin started planting trees on the Hyde Park estate to also make his forest a profitable venture. His words express another motive, "I don't suppose there is anything in nature that I am so fond of as trees." To prove the point, by the time of his death more than 370,000 trees had been planted on a thousand acres of his estate, 800 acres of natural growth forest land and 250 acres of plantations.[10] Among them were thousands of Christmas trees.

A Christmas tree plantation of Norway spruce came into being at Hyde Park in 1926. The trees were planted on poor rocky soil and spaced a little over three feet apart. Ten years later 150 trees were cut from this four-acre plot for the Christmas season and by 1940, 3,600 trees had been cut and sold.

William Plog, Superintendent of F.D.R.'s Hyde Park Estate, with a ruler to show the height of Christmas trees. Courtesy Franklin D. Roosevelt Library, Hyde Park, New York

Other plots were planted to expand Christmas tree sales. As trees were cut, the open places were replanted to gain a continual yield of trees. Thirty thousand trees including Norway spruce, Balsam fir, Canadian White spruce, and Douglas fir were ordered for planting in the spring of 1944.

William Plog, Superintendent of the Hyde Park Estate, was asked to get some help to trim the brush around the Christmas trees and cut off long leaders and wide branches to make the trees more attractive to buyers. Prospective buyers had the opportunity to visit Hyde Park to inspect the Christmas trees.

In 1943, letters from Grace G. Tully, Private Secretary to the President, offered the entire crop of Norway spruce, Canadian White spruce, and Balsam fir to A & P Food Stores, Safeway Stores, Bloomingdale's, R. H. Macy, and several other companies.[11] The best offer was made by the Atlantic Commission Company for thirty-five hundred trees which required intensive cutting in every plot. The President was pleased when he received a check from Mr. Plog for the sale of these trees.

The next year the President himself wrote the letters. After offering to have Mr. Plog show the trees, the President wrote that the trees were from three to six feet and over in height and "mostly Norway spruce, with a rough estimate of fifteen hundred available; there are 60 to 100 Balsam fir trees; about 100 Douglas fir trees; and if you desire table trees, the total could run up to 2500 to 3000." The trees were to be delivered to the buyers' trucks with branches tied and the President suggested "that it will pay to have these trees cut as late as possible to insure good condition on December 25th." The Atlantic Commission Company was again the successful bidder.

Christmas trees also became a way for the President to forge closer bonds with his allies in the total war to defeat Hitler. In a memorandum to Grace Tully, the President wrote on October 18, 1943, "Take up with General Arnold and find out what is the latest date that I can deliver a Christmas tree for Winston Churchill and send it over by a bomber or otherwise in order to reach him at Chequiers, England, before Christmas." A tree was also sent to the Crown Princess of Norway at Bethesda, Maryland, whose country was at this time occupied by German forces.

Franklin D. Roosevelt died a month before the end of the war on April 12, 1945, about the time his Christmas tree seedlings were being planted. He was returned to Hyde Park where he so often enjoyed inspecting his forests and tree plantations in his manually controlled automobile. The coffin was borne up the trail through his beloved woods from the railroad siding bordering the Hudson River to the beautiful Rose Garden where he and Mrs. Roosevelt are buried today.

Abraczinskas Plantations

The contributions of Andrew Abraczinskas became the foundation for a large Christmas tree enterprise. The entire family joined in to make it all happen. Sons Evon and Anthony, known as Duke, and Andrew's sister, Helen, played a major role. In 1950, Duke Abraczinskas planted over a hundred acres of Douglas fir and in the two decades that followed more than fifteen hundred acres were planted with over two million trees. The family expanded in size with grandchildren and then great grandchildren and so did the number of acres and trees. Today, the Abraczinskas Nurseries, Inc., operated by five of Andrew's great-grandchildren, has more than twenty-five hundred acres with several million Christmas trees.

The Roosevelt family with Christmas tree in White House, 1939.
Courtesy Franklin D. Roosevelt Library, Hyde Park, New York

Hofert Plantations

Hofert had built a large market that extended across the country and into Canada, and supplied it with wild trees from forests throughout his territory. In addition, thousands of acres of land were purchased in the southern region of Puget Sound for Christmas tree production. About half of this land was gradually converted to plantations and additional acres acquired for expansion.

John H. Hofert was joined in his company by two sons, Alvin and Milton, and a daughter, Esther and husband, Lyall F. Scott. Later a member of the third generation, John A. Hofert, began to take an active part in the business. Several years before Alvin died in 1989, Scott C. Scott, the grandson of Lyall, became the manager. In 1992, the family decided to sell the assets of the J. Hofert Company after 112 years in the industry. Harold "Hal" Schudel of the Holiday Tree Farm in Oregon acquired 1762 acres of land owned and leased by Hofert including a total of 1,629,000 trees.[12] Hofert land in several states and Canadian provinces is under lease to other producers, some of whom still harvest Christmas trees.

Alvin H. Hofert and son, John A. Hofert.

The Kirk Wautoma Plantation

In 1953, the Kirks began to buy deserted farms in flat lands near Wautoma, Wisconsin. Spanning more than ten thousand acres, the Wautoma Plantation is today the largest of the Kirk operations. The plantation is a group of some 115 separate farms, each of which is planted with a particular species of tree such as Scotch pine, Fraser fir, Balsam fir, White pine, and Blue spruce. The glaciers brought a mixture of loams, clays, and silts, but most of the soil is sandy in which Scotch pine trees thrive particularly well.

The farms are named, numbered, and planted in rotation so that each farm has trees of one age. "We grow Christmas trees like farmers grow corn, only trees take from seven to ten years to harvest," explains Gary Nelson, the production manager in Wisconsin. Twenty-four full-time and as many as six hundred part-time workers are employed. The advantage of plantations over the forests is that cultivation, fertilization, shearing, and cutting can be done more economically. It is easier to maintain high quality so important in large volume production. More than four hundred thousand Scotch and White pines, Blue spruce, Balsam and Fraser firs are shipped each year to customers in thirty-five states in the Midwest, south, and east. For the western markets, Douglas and Noble fir trees are grown on plantations in the states of Oregon and Washington. "When my grandfather and father started the business most of our Christmas trees came from forests," says Rick Kirk, the company president, "today they are grown on plantations."

Japanese Bombs Create a Disaster for Christmas Trees

Every year for many decades the people of Hawaii have received their annual supply of Christmas trees through what is believed to be the single biggest waterborne shipment of its kind in the world. Paul Kirk, who played a major role in developing this market, recalls a dramatic incident during an early year of this annual sojourn. Christmas trees were piled high on the deck of the ship that was one day out of Honolulu. The date was December 7, 1941, "a day which will live in infamy" to quote Franklin D. Roosevelt, President and Christmas tree farmer. Japanese bombers had attacked Pearl Harbor and sunk a large part of the American navy.

The Christmas tree ship turned around and headed back home. As it approached the northwest coast during the night, all lights were out to escape detection by the Japanese. Suddenly, the ship hit a sand bar near the Columbia River jarring loose the protective tarps over the trees. The trees rolled off the ship and the tides delivered them up and down the coast just in time for the Christmas holiday.

It begins with Christmas tree growers in the Pacific Northwest and ends with the arrival of the "Christmas tree ship" in Honolulu. "Typically," says Ronald Barrett, sales manager of the Matson Navigation Line, "the bulk of the trees arrive on Thursday, Thanksgiving Day, and are available for sale by the following day."

Loading Christmas trees for shipment overseas.

Oregon provides about 80 percent of the trees for Hawaii and the remainder come from the Olympic Peninsula near Seattle. Several large suppliers and dozens of smaller growers participate in the shipment. Much planning and coordination are involved. "It starts with the suppliers," says Bill Williams, Matson inland operation manager. "The shippers choose the truckers they want to use, tell us when they will start cutting and when they will start to move the trees." Thousands of cut trees are bundled and then placed on a conveyer belt that takes them into large containers. A computer is used to plan the placement of the containers on the ship and a special electrical system is necessary for the many refrigerated containers (called reefers). Dale Palmer, vessel superintendent, emphasizes, "There is also quite a large variance between temperatures in Seattle and in Honolulu, which means the reefers have to be closely monitored."

The Christmas trees arrive in four main shipments, the first in the middle of November, primarily for store

G. R. and Paul Kirk featured on the cover of Business Week. Reprinted from December 15, 1956 issue of Business Week by special permission. © 1956 by McGraw-Hill Companies.

displays and the neighboring islands. The traditional "Christmas tree ship" with a symbolic tree tied to her mast normally docks on Thanksgiving Day with the rest of the trees arriving early in December. Department of Agriculture inspectors check the trees in each container for such unwanted pests as wasps.

Schedules are highly important because many trees are pre-sold and the retailers need to inform their customers on arrival times. The selling of almost two hundred thousand Christmas trees shipped there has been called an 'annual adventure'.

Special Recognition for the Kirks

In 1956, G. R. and Paul Kirk were featured on the cover of *Business Week* magazine and given special recognition for their achievements. They had built one of the largest Christmas tree companies in the world, harvesting and marketing trees all across the continent, and abroad. Father and son had played complementary yet different roles in bringing it all about. G. R. remained in the corporate offices in Tacoma giving administrative support to son Paul who couldn't sit still. Paul was always at the front lines developing new markets, finding new forests and trees, and improving operations. His dynamic personality and drive created a rate of company growth that constantly challenged G. R.'s administrative skills.

As a rival they recognized only the J. Hofert Company of Los Angeles, their primary competitor for more than 70 years. The two continued to compete until the Hofert Company ceased to exist in 1992. The Kirk Company remains as a leading company in a changed industry.

Beyond the Early Pioneers

Many others have built upon the legacy left by the early pioneers. Initiative and just plain hard work continue to play an important part in the industry. Like many of those from the past, several generations of family are frequently involved.

Seeking Green Gold

A comment by his college professor, "Christmas trees are green gold," caused George Frelk to buy a small farm in 1955 to try to prove the point. His brother, Calvin Frelk, joined him and the two built a large tree farm in Wisconsin. In 1973, Calvin and wife Arlene became the sole owners by buying George's interests. Later they formed a family partnership with their daughter, Ginger, and husband John Ahl, the Northern Christmas Tree Growers, which today has more than six thousand acres of Christmas trees, timber, and nursery plants. Green gold that came from hard work.

Christmas Trees Instead of an Emerald Ring

Erin Fleck of the Emerald Christmas Tree Farm in Washington reports that her father, Jack Fleck, gave his new bride, Mary Ann, an emerging Christmas tree farm as a wedding gift, "it was that or an emerald ring . . . he couldn't afford both, so the trees were it." Jack Fleck, who in his later years looked like a Santa Claus with twinkling blue eyes, a chuckle, and a white beard, played a major role in the industry shipping as many as a million trees. On their 25th wedding anniversary, Jack presented Mary Ann with a beautiful emerald ring. After his death in 1991, two daughters, Erin and Meaghan, manage the company for their mother.

Moving Christmas Trees Indian Style

Thomas and Joan Beutell farm 750 acres of Fraser firs on several mountains about forty-five miles southwest of Asheville, North Carolina. During the early years, Thomas developed a unique technique for moving Christmas trees down a mountain and experienced more than a little exercise in the process. He would walk up the mountain for two miles, cut a few Fraser firs, place them between the two poles of a travois, a device used by the Plains Indians, and then move them down the mountain. The trees were taken by truck to Atlanta which is still a major market for Beutell Fraser firs. To improve the quality of their Fraser firs, the Beutells expanded their operations to include a nursery that has the benefit of three seed orchards. Their company, the Wolf Tree Farm and Nursery, Inc., has become a family enterprise with son, Thomas Jr. and daughter, Renee, and their spouses playing an active part.

After Pumpkins for Halloween Come Trees for Christmas

In the late sixties, to supplement the income from his dairy farm in Oregon, Robert Hoffman began doing some work for the J. Hofert Company. At the end of a day of planting on Hofert land, Bob would ask Alvin Hofert what he should do with the seedlings that were left over. "Take them home," said Alvin, "and plant them on your farm."

After a time there were enough trees on the Hoffman farm to warrant Bob's full attention. Today, Hoffman Trees has more than a thousand acres of trees with an annual harvest of 100 to 150 thousand trees. Many of them go to wholesalers but Bob takes a personal hand in retailing a sizable number. Every October for many years he has traveled to Los Angeles to first sell several truckloads of pumpkins for Halloween and then retail his trees for Christmas.

In addition to pumpkins and trees, the Hoffmans grow vegetables and flowers. Daughter, Julie, serves as office manager and son, Steven, as production manager. Their office is a house built in 1907 by Bob's grandfather who came from Virginia.

Forests of Wild Elk and Trees

During a hunting trip for elk in 1954, Harold "Hal" Schudel and Paul Goodmonson decided to earn some extra income selling Christmas trees. For the first few years they cut wild trees on the logged over land owned by timber companies and sold them in local markets. In 1957 the two began to purchase land to plant and cultivate large numbers of the highly popular Douglas firs for an expanded market. Hal Schudel bought Paul Goodmonson's interest in 1972 and reorganized as a family enterprise involving his sons. Thousands of acres were added to the Schudel enterprise, including land formerly owned by the J. Hofert Company, creating one of the largest companies in the United States. From a total inventory of over 6.5 million trees on eight thousand acres of land, Schudel's Holiday Tree Farms, Inc. of Corvallis, Oregon, shipped out nearly a million trees during a recent year.

A Friendly Takeover

Not to be outdone, in 1976 Paul Goodmonson joined Robert Stohr, Fred Peste, and Gary Bishop in a consortium to buy the twelve hundred acre tree plantation owned by the Crown Zellerbach Company for a reported three million dollars. The new company was named Noble Mountain Tree Farm with offices in Salem, Oregon. Robert Schaefer, a former employee of Crown Zellerbach was appointed to serve as the operating manager. Paul Goodmonson became the first managing partner and after he retired in 1984, Robert Stohr assumed his position.

Oil Paintings for a Carload of Christmas Trees

Clarence Stohr, an insurance executive, moved from Los Angeles to Washington State for reasons of health. He enjoyed working in the woods which prompted an interest in the Christmas tree business. With five hundred dollars his wife, Billy, had saved selling her oil paintings, Clarence made a down payment on a carload of trees which he sold for a good profit in the Los Angeles market. This beginning gave rise to a family partnership which later included Fred Peste, an old hand in the business.

Clarence's son, Robert, graduated from the University of Washington Law School and became a member of the Washington State Bar. He felt almost guilty when he turned down a position in a prominent law firm to pursue his true passion, the Christmas tree business. His wife, Joy, describes the early years, "Bob was a great salesman but he hated being away from his family so I became involved in sales. We packed up our two children, Stephanie and Brandt, and traveled up and down the coast seeing customers and selling Christmas trees." Like the Hoferts, the Kirks, and Clarence Stohr before them, Bob and Joy sold trees out of railroad cars at the 8th and Alameda train tracks in Los Angeles. As Joy recalls, "Bob and I remembered those days very nostalgically."

Noble Mountain Tree Farm, Salem, Oregon.

The Stohr and Peste partnership was highly successful and after a time was selling far more trees than it could possibly produce. The problem was partly solved with the trees that became available through the Crown Zellerbach purchase. The Stohrs became the sole owners of the Douglas Fir Christmas Tree Company and launched a major expansion program by buying land and planting trees at a rapid pace. With the help of their dedicated employees, they overcame many obstacles including one of the worst snow storms in Washington state history. A new office complex was built and the production process completely modernized. The Douglas Fir Christmas Tree Company has become a giant in its own right, which together with their ownership in the Noble Mountain Tree Farm, placed the Stohrs among the largest producers in the industry.

A sad sequel to this story occurred in 1996. A dog jumped out in front of Bob Stohr's car and to avoid hitting him, Bob swerved sharply and the car flipped over. Bob died from injuries suffered in that accident but, "Thank God," he might well have said, "my dog Bear riding with me in the car was spared." A memorial service was held for Robert Clarence Stohr in the church where he and Joy were married.

Baby Boomers Are Different People

Gary Riessen of the Mathisen Tree Farms and Fairplains Nursery in Michigan has given a great deal of thought to the future.[13] Speaking from the vantage point of both his company and the industry, Riessen stresses the importance of planning for a future of uncertainty and change. Production efficiencies to reduce the cost per tree will become increasingly important as both labor and land costs rise. The optimum size of companies and the structure of the market will change significantly. Demographics will play a major role. Aging "baby boomers" will live differently than their parents of the same age and are likely to demand taller trees for vaulted ceilings, trees for several rooms, and trees as a part of landscaping. Greater emphasis on quality and exotic species can be expected.

Stand Straight and Tall

The small Michigan farm purchased by Carl Wahmhoff in 1955 is now a third generation family enterprise with eight hundred acres of land, four retail lots, a choose and cut farm, and a nursery.

Wahmhoff Farms also manufactures a stand that displays a tree securely and perfectly straight in seconds, even if the trunk is crooked.

Grapes, Cattle, or Christmas Trees

Jean Collins in Oklahoma bought a little land and then wondered what to do with it.[14] "I investigated grapes, cattle, Christmas trees, everything," she said. Her decision was Christmas trees and through persistence and hard work she developed a thriving business, recently adding 2,750 trees. She hires seasonal help including her 71 year old mother, Ruth Roberts, who helps with mowing and shearing.

On the Top of Pond Mountain

Dale and Ruth Shepherd in North Carolina knew that they were going to grow Fraser firs when they bought their first hundred acres of land in 1968. Over the years they expanded the number of acres and trees. The Shepherds reached new heights with a plantation of fifteen hundred acres more than four thousand feet high on Pond Mountain.

The Christmas Tree Industry

Today, there are about twelve thousand growers in the United States who produce trees on about a million acres and employ more than one hundred thousand people on a full and part-time basis. Some producers are large, growing five to ten million Christmas trees and harvesting up to a million. Somewhat down the scale in size are the plantations with a hundred thousand to five hundred thousand trees. In addition, there are many companies that grow from twenty thousand to a hundred thousand trees. Five thousand growers have sought to rekindle an earlier tradition by permitting families to choose and cut their own trees.

In recent years, well over thirty-five million Christmas trees have been annually grown in North American both for the domestic market and export.[15] The manner in which this supply is produced has changed dramatically. In the late 1940's, more than 90 percent of Christmas trees were still wild trees from forests and other types of land with less than 10 percent from plantations. Today, more than 90 percent of the trees are grown on plantations and the remainder are "wild" trees, most of which are extensively cultivated and pruned.

As the number of growers increased in a state or region, a few would meet periodically on an informal basis. Others joined in and as the few became many, Christmas tree grower associations began to appear. Pennsylvania formed the first in 1944 which was followed by eighteen states and regions during the 1950's. Soon they began to recognize that many problems were industry-wide and required cooperation among associations. The National Christmas Tree Growers Association was formed in September of 1955. Beginning with eight state associations, the number of charter members has extended into thirty-five state and regional associations. A list of some of the people who play an administrative role in these associations can be found on pages 88 and 89.

The quality of Christmas trees has improved dramatically through intensive cultivation, quality seedlings and transplants, disease and insect control, and skillful shearing. Simultaneously, the harvesting and marketing of trees has become more efficient with innovative tools, machinery, and transport. These developments and practices are now considered.

CHRISTMAS TREE FORESTS AND FARMS

Old, even in geologic time, the ancestor of the Christmas tree appeared 285 million years ago when all of the land was still joined in one continent called Pangaea. Conifer forests flourished in the warm climate and rainy weather, and for 150 million years dinosaurs called them home. Pangaea split into five continents and the dinosaurs disappeared. The conifers continued to thrive in much of the world including North America.

Improving upon Nature

Conifers as Christmas Trees

Most conifers bear cones and are evergreen, but only some species become Christmas trees. Among these are the cedars, cypresses, firs, pines, and spruces, each of which has developed subspecies that depart from the norm. In the wild they adapt to variations in soil and climate and compete for space with other trees including their own kind. Cones provide a continual supply of seeds for new ventures in survival. Bushes, grasses, and other plants stand in the way. Animals who eat and trample can also stop their lease on life. Then man steps into this natural milieu to cut Christmas trees.

Christmas trees in a Canadian forest.

The Early Years

During the early years most of the Christmas trees in North America were wild trees from forests and other naturally seeded places. Trees were selected for shape and size, cut, sorted, and tied into bundles, and then moved by oxen or horse-drawn wagons to railway cars or ships destined for wholesalers and retailers.

Wild Trees Can Be Improved

High levels of cutting combined with a rapidly growing demand for Christmas trees created a need to improve upon nature. As President Franklin D. Roosevelt pointed out, "While only God can make a tree, we have to do a little bit to help ourselves." Removing unwanted plants and thinning the wild trees gives them more room to grow. Fertilizing and spraying for disease and insects are helpful. Basal pruning and shearing make the wild tree a better looking Christmas tree. Through these techniques the wild trees in forests continue to provide beautiful Christmas trees.

Christmas Tree Plantations

In recent years most of the Christmas trees in North America have been grown on plantations. Keith Jacobs, a Minnesota tree grower, points out "that Christmas trees are the same as any other agricultural

Christmas tree plantation, Sandpoint, Idaho. Courtesy Carol and Dave Jenkins

Christmas tree plantation, North Carolina. Courtesy Dale Shepherd

Cones which contain the seeds for growing trees. Courtesy Silvaseed

Conifer seeds from which seedlings are grown. Courtesy Silvaseed

crop. These trees are raised to be cut as Christmas trees. The people who think that a vital national resource is destroyed when millions of Christmas trees are cut are wrong." Every tree that is cut is replaced with one or more new trees.

Matching Species, Soil, and Weather

Christmas trees can be grown on soils and terrain where other crops cannot survive. Not any old plot will do. Tree growers need to select species that are right for the kinds of soil on their plantations. Firs do not grow well in wet and heavy clay soil while Scotch pines thrive on most soils, loamy, clay, or rocky. Acidity or alkalinity makes a difference, and trees grow better with sufficient humus and nutrients.

Although not much can be done to change the weather, tree growers select the kinds of trees that are suited for the climate in their regions. Scotch pines grow better in dry areas than Balsam and Douglas firs. The adaptability of trees to sunshine and temperature is important.

From Seed Cones to Seedlings

Most people are familiar with conifer cones. If there is no frost damage in the spring, the trees develop cones every two or three years. When the cones mature they break open and the winged seeds are dispersed. The wind can take them far afield. Wild trees in forests and other natural settings are constantly replenished in this way. Only a few seeds germinate but sheer numbers assure the survival of the species. This natural process can be duplicated and even improved.

Cones are usually gathered in the early fall when they are about ready to open, covered with pitch and quite sticky. After drying, a little shaking will make the seed drop out, wing and all. Since man and not nature will do the planting, the wings are usually removed and the seeds cleaned by winnowing. At this point they can be stored for a short time or planted in especially prepared seed beds to promote growth and survival. It takes one to three years to grow seedlings which are often transplanted for another year or two. Pine seedlings are sometimes sturdy enough for field planting with transplants best for fir and spruce.

Seedlings can also be grown as plugs in small plastic containers within a controlled greenhouse environment, and then transplanted before subjecting them to the rigors of the field. Plugs cost more than bare soil seedlings but offer greater uniformity and better stems.

Nurseries for Quality Christmas Trees

Probably the most important technique for improving quality is to select seed from superior trees in terms of shape, color, and needle form. Many larger companies maintain seed tree orchards and sometimes operate both as nurseries and tree plantations. Few of the smaller tree growers gather their own seed and grow seedlings and transplants. One exception is Earl Worthington in Georgia who collects seed from his select trees and raises his own seedlings. Improved seed is also developed through cooperative effort. The Maine Christmas Tree Association has two seed orchards with fifty parent trees to develop a premium six-foot Maine Balsam fir.[1]

Most growers obtain their seedlings and transplants from nurseries, some of which offer a wide range of species and others a more limited number suitable for particular regions. Larger nurseries grow seedlings from the seed of superior trees grown abroad, such as the French Alpine region, the Burgos or Guaderrama Mountains of Spain, and the Bavarian forests. State agricultural experiment stations and their counterparts in Canada have also helped develop superior trees. Nurseries generally provide data about the kind of soil and climate that are best for the species they offer.

Cloning Superior Trees

Portions of a tree are grafted upon a root of another tree to produce exact copies or clones. Such asexual or vegetative propagation makes possible the reproduction of superior trees and helps assure an adequate supply of superior seed. It is especially important in reproducing hybrids because seed from plants grown from hybrid seed cannot generally be used for reseeding.

The Search for Exotic Conifers

There is a constant search for exotic conifers that offer potential for the future. Besides those that might be found in North America, species growing in such places as Korea, Manchuria, and China hold promise for an improved Christmas tree.[2] Dean Swift from Colorado drove over three thousand miles through spruce and fir territory before finding the Swift Silver Concolor fir, a rapidly growing tree with silver-blue needles. Others have focused attention upon the Bracted fir of Nova Scotia that may have qualities for a superior tree. Gary Riessen has experimented with Corkbark fir and Korean fir and feels that they have qualities that could lead to an improved tree. Bob Girardin, a specialist in exotic trees, and Riessen recommend experimentation and trial plantings.[3]

Plugs or seedlings grown in small plastic containers. Courtesy Silvaseed

Seedlings planted in prepared beds become transplants, such as those shown here, for planting in fields. Courtesy Richard Downey

Success does not come easily but when it does the result can be dramatic. A good example is the Nordmann fir which originated in the mountainous areas of the eastern end of the Black Sea. Introduced into Denmark in the middle of the last century, the Nordmann fir has become a highly popular Christmas tree in Europe. Randy and Jim Bays of Oregon feel that this tree has great potential for the United States.[4]

Better Christmas Trees Through Mutation

A tree can become a better tree through mutation, a heritable alteration in genes or chromosomes. However, the good qualities that arise are often negated by bad ones. Mutation has a failure rate of at least 90 percent. The people who search for exotic trees are ever hopeful that somewhere in the world there is a tree that has beaten these odds and that they will find it.

A New Tree From a London Arboretum

Better quality trees have also resulted from the development of hybrids through cross-pollination. The Leyland cypress is such a tree. At a London arboretum in 1888, the accidental cross pollination of the Alaska cedar and the Monterey cypress resulted in the Leyland cypress which gained the best characteristics of both parents. About the only negative quality is a lack of fragrance. After additional experimentation at Clemson University, the Leyland cypress has become

an important Christmas tree in the South. Bill Murray, a Georgia nurseryman and tree grower, has said, "The Leyland cypress is a beautiful and sturdy tree with no natural enemies."

Growing Quality Christmas Trees

Spring is the Season for Planting

There is no one best way to grow Christmas trees. Some growers create a setting similar to that found in nature by planting seedlings or transplants in sod. Keeping out the weeds and mowing the grass are ways to give an advantage to the trees. Fertilizers and herbicides can tip the scales even further, however, growers interested in organic farming skip the chemicals.

At the other extreme are tree growers who imitate corn farmers by planting in bare soil maintained through cultivation and chemicals. Many larger growers mass produce millions of Christmas trees in this way. This kind of production is efficient and cost effective and has become increasingly important in a highly competitive industry.

Some growers limit soil tillage to plowing furrows into which trees are planted. The nature of the terrain and the kind of soil can make a difference. A hilly landscape or rocky and gravelly soil creates special planting and cultivation problems.

Continuous Production and Marketing

Christmas tree farmers attempt to develop a system of continuous production and marketing. Although the average growth rate for a six foot tree is about seven years, planning is made more difficult by varied rates for different species which can range from four to fifteen years. A related problem is that a row or field of trees is often harvested over a period of several years. Trees planted on the same day with good planting stock should be ready to harvest at the same

Planting seedlings in the field.

time. In actual practice, some trees will have lagged behind in growth and others will be deficient in other ways. One solution is to cut them all and destroy the trees that are not salable. Another is to harvest over a period of two or three years to give extra time for trees to fill out or gain height. The trees that still lack sufficient quality are eliminated with the stumps.

Rather than wait for this point to be reached, some growers simply replant the spaces vacated by the harvested trees which can lead to a haphazard distribution of different sized trees. Such an approach can be suitable for a choose and cut farm, but creates problems for large plantations. A good solution is to develop fields of sizes that make for efficient planting, cultivating, and harvesting with rotations based on the average number of years required for particular species.

A Million Trees a Mile

Planting trees too close gives height but makes them too scrawny for Christmas trees. A recommended spacing for five to seven foot spruce and firs is 5 by 5 feet and for pines 6 by 6 feet. It is possible to grow a million trees on a square mile of land although the actual number is usually somewhat lower. On one large plantation the rows are set six feet apart with a spacing of five and one-half feet for the trees in each row. A half foot means more than a hundred additional trees per acre!

Muscle and Machine Power

Spring is the best planting time but transplants with a good root system have been successfully planted in the fall. Planting can be done with a spade or a planting bar, good shoe soles, and muscle power. The planting bar is thrust into the soil, moved back and forth a little to create a slit into which the seedling or transplant is inserted. A little scraping of the shoe closes the hole and a stomp or two firms the soil. These tasks can be performed cooperatively by two or three persons to speed the process. The reason for doing it all with some dispatch is pointed out by tree grower Lewis Hill, "I used to tell my helpers to think of the trees as trout and never leave the roots exposed to air for more than a short time or they would die."[5]

When the terrain is right, a planting machine with a two- or three-person crew can greatly increase the number of trees planted. The trees are normally planted in long rows with a prescribed distance between trees and rows. Access roads for trucks and equipment and space for harvesting the trees are usually a part of the layout. Such spacing can do double service as firebreaks.

Several thousand trees per day can be planted by hand. Machines can increase the total to more than ten thousand. In a large Wisconsin plantation the number is raised to twenty thousand a day by using two machines manned by two persons doing the planting and someone in the middle handing out the moist transplants.

Growing Trees From Stumps

Although most Christmas trees are grown from seed, seedlings, and transplants, they can also be grown from the stumps of previously cut trees, thereby gaining the advantage of an established root system. It generally takes less time to grow a tree from stumps and can be less costly on a tree by tree basis. A small number of growers produce trees in this way, often only to replace a few trees that didn't make it or to experiment with special trees on a special plot of land. Stump culture is not efficient for larger tree growers and generally cannot be sustained economically.

In northern Wisconsin Paul Schroeder is one of the few, if not the only tree grower, who has gained a unique benefit from stump culture. He grazes 150 head

A close view of the planting process. Photographed by W. L. Coffman

of fat cows with calves among his 120 thousand Balsam fir trees to keep the grass and other competitive plants down. The cattle do use the trees as rubbing posts and fly swatters which ruin the lower branches. There is little harm but only because Schroeder cuts his trees several feet above the ground and uses the stumps to grow new trees.[6]

Summer Toil Brings Christmas Joy

Bob Scott, tree farmer and President of the National Christmas Tree Association, emphasizes that "much work and patience go into every tree. From the time the tree is first planted in the ground to the day it is decorated, it needs to be sheared, pruned, fertilized and protected from pests and diseases."

It is not always easy to apply the right amount of lime and fertilizers for a good crop of trees. Too much is as bad as too little. Not only is money wasted but the trees can be damaged. The weather is always a problem. Too much rain or too little rain, large hail stones, and a wind storm can take a heavy toll. A corn or wheat farmer risks losing a part of and even his entire crop for one year. For the Christmas tree farmer a single disaster can destroy his crop for many years.

Hand spraying to control disease, harmful insects, or weeds.

An Army of Insects

Trees are no less subject to the ravages of bacteria and viruses than human beings and the diagnosis is often equally difficult. They also have symptoms such as wilted or discolored foliage. A literal army of insects is ever ready to chew or spread disease. There are aphids, budworms, grubs, mites, sawflies, webworms, and many more. Fungi attack roots, needles, and trunks and little worms called nematodes are often not far behind.

Trees that are well cultivated and have sufficient nutrients are less likely to succumb to disease. The damage can often be reduced by removing the diseased plants to save the healthy ones. If all else fails a long list of chemicals is available to destroy the troublesome pests.

Fertilizers and pesticides are often applied with hand-held spreaders and tank sprayers, but engine-powered equipment mounted on trucks and tractors become necessary in large scale operations. Airplanes and helicopters speed the process.

Weeds can be controlled by mowing and cultivation, but herbicides are commonly used when trees are planted on bare soil. Walk-behind and riding mowers are available to cut weeds and grass and mechanized cultivators to facilitate bare soil growing.

Spraying with an airplane.

Chemicals work miracles for trees, but they can be hazardous if improperly handled. Special equipment, protective clothing, and constant warnings reduce the danger.

Animals Eat, Rub, and Trample

Animals can create havoc with Christmas trees. In some regions deer are a real problem, in others moose and elk head the list. A few states provide compensation for animal damage but Christmas trees are often excluded.

Arlene Frelk in Wisconsin reports that beavers dam creeks and flood the land. Small mice gnaw on the bark, squirrels like terminal buds, and rabbits eat almost everything. "Blackbirds land on the leaders and break them, a real nuisance," reports Dan Hoffman in Iowa. Adding insult to injury, the birds sometimes dive bomb Dan when he gets too close to their nests.

Domesticated animals such as cattle and horses can cause damage by trampling upon the trees or rubbing against them. They are not inclined to browse on evergreen foliage if there is enough grass or legumes. Exceptions can be expensive.

A promotional plan was to photograph Kirk Company trees in a pastoral setting with Mount Rainier in the background. To do so a variety of species were brought at considerable cost from distant places in the United States and Canada and set up in a pasture for a photographic session the next morning. When the photographers arrived, the cattle had stripped every tree.

Tree Poachers Exact a Toll

On occasion people steal trees for their homes or many trees for sale and profit. Tree poachers who take out truckloads of Christmas trees have become a major problem in federal and state forests. Some are caught but most are not. Tree plantations face similar problems. Lewis Hill saw a parked shiny new Oldsmobile by the side of the road and spotted a woman in a mink coat busily sawing down one of his trees.[7] He asked her if she also planned to steal her Christmas turkey. She responded in an unfriendly manner and with a loud voice claimed that she didn't know the tree belonged to anyone.

The Hazard of Fire

Besides firebreaks created by roadways and other spacing, standby fire fighting equipment might have helped Henry and Phyllis Kroeker in the spring of 1996.[8] In spite of Governor Bill Graves "no burning" edict, someone decided to burn trash. Pushed by strong winds the fire spread rapidly through a wide swath of Kansas countryside endangering many homes and destroying all of the 1,500 Scotch and Austrian pines owned by the Kroekers. Careless people are a constant hazard to hard working Christmas tree growers. A toss of a cigarette can destroy the work of many years.

Pruning and Shearing Trees

Pruning and shearing can significantly improve the appearance of Christmas trees in both natural and plantation settings. Pruning creates a better tree by cutting away unwanted branches, especially the thin and scrawny branches at the bottom. Shearing cuts back new soft foliar growth. For pine trees shearing stimulates the tip to form more buds thereby creating more branches and greater density. Spruce and fir trees also have buds along their branches that create greater density and makes them easier to shape. Pines are usually sheared every year for at least four years with fewer shearings for spruce and fir trees. The goal is a more beautiful Christmas tree.

Shearing can be done with a sixteen-inch knife or machete wielded by a strong arm tree after tree after tree. Dan Hoffman in Iowa talked about the three weeks in June he shears his twenty-two thousand trees. He commented, "Good exercise, but hard work, especially when the temperature climbs above ninety degrees. It must be done if my customers are to have nicely shaped trees." The number of trees sheared in larger plantations can be counted in the millions.

How many trees can be sheared in a day? With a knife the number may vary from several hundred to a thousand trees depending on the skills of the shearer. Hand pruners and hedge shears take more time. With a mechanized shearing machine strapped on the shoulders of the operator or mounted on a cart, the number can be increased significantly. An average

Pruning branches for a better shaped tree.

operator can shear from fifteen hundred to twenty-five hundred trees in a six-hour day. The perseverance of the operator, the size and kind of tree, and customer preferences make a difference.

Dan Hoffman shearing Christmas trees with a 16-inch knife. Photographed by Marlene Lucas, courtesy Cedar Rapids Gazette

Group shearing at large Christmas tree plantation with crews of five or six workers and supervisor.

The Time to Harvest

Harvest time brings more hard work and a challenge. Christmas tree growers face a seemingly impossible task of delivering millions of trees to customers in a matter of weeks. The trees to be cut are tagged for harvesting in mid-November. Colored plastic ribbons indicate the species, size in feet, and grade of each tree ranging from premium to standard. Some trees, hopefully only a few, are not salable.

A colorant that gives a natural appearance and does not come off is often sprayed on pine trees. The film formed on the needles screens out ultraviolet rays, a major cause of chlorosis or yellowing.

For plantations marketing Christmas trees to wholesale and retail customers, harvesting begins in November. The exact date varies with the climate in different states and provinces such as North Carolina, Wisconsin, Oregon, and British Columbia. Also important is the species to be harvested. Gary Riessen reports that at the Mathisen Tree Farms in Michigan Scotch pine are harvested first, then Fraser fir followed by Douglas fir, and the last to be cut are the Balsam firs and Colorado blue spruce.[9] The reason

The trees to be cut are tagged with colored plastic ribbons to indicate species, size in feet, and grade.

Cutting trees.

Helicopters can be used to move a large number of trees in a short time.

Balers compact trees and wrap them in twine or polyethylene netting to facilitate storage and transportation.

for this sequence is that pines are most hardy after harvesting and spruce the least. Tagged trees are cut, cleaned, baled, and temporarily held in storage until shipment begins.

Trees can be cut with bow saws, chain saws, brush cutters, or mechanized cutting equipment. In one large plantation in Wisconsin as many as twenty-five thousand trees are cut in a day. To facilitate transport and prevent damage, balers compact trees by wrapping them in twine or polyethylene netting. For even better space utilization for storage and transport, trees are palletized, a process first utilized by Yule Tree Farms and Silver Mountain Christmas Trees, both located in Oregon.

"Growers have developed methods of storing trees so that they retain their moisture and are still fresh when purchased by the consumer," says Bob Scott. Trees are stored in sheds covered for shade and lined on the bottom with sawdust. Water is sprayed on them every evening to assure that the moisture content remains the same as when they were cut.

Much sorting by species, size, grade, and customer orders takes place throughout harvesting. Specialized trailers, wagons, conveyer belts, and elevators for loading are designed for efficiency and cost reduction. When roads do not exist or are inadequate, helicopters are sometimes used to move trees. They may also offer a cost advantage by speeding the harvest and reducing manpower needs. Jim Heater of Silver Mountain Christmas Trees and Bob Schaefer of Noble Mountain Tree Farm, who first used helicopters for this purpose, report that from eight to ten thousand trees are normally moved in a day but the number has been increased to sixteen thousand for short distances.

The trees are loaded on trucks to transport them to wholesalers and retailers throughout the country. For some larger companies a thousand or more trucks are needed. The ships that take trees to Hawaii and Puerto Rico are equipped to accommodate the need for moisture and right temperature.

What happens to stumps? Rotary stump grinders can be used to remove most of the upper portions after which a disk contends with the remaining roots. Jim Heater reports that his company has developed a two row cutter which lowers the stumps and generally cleans debris from clear-cut fields. Sometimes a heavy

A storage facility sometimes used during the harvest season. The trees are sprayed with water every evening to keep them as fresh as when they were first cut.

A conveyer is being used to load trees on a truck.

disking is all that is required, especially after two or three years. Pines are less of a problem than firs. New trees are frequently planted between the old rows with stumps and roots left to decompose. Another technique is to plant a different crop such as corn for a couple of years.

The People on Christmas Tree Plantations

"I work the year-round," says Ruth Taylor of the Manners Christmas Tree Farm in New Lyme, Ohio, "there's a constant flow of different things at different times."[10] In addition to such managerial functions as budgeting and scheduling, Taylor often joins her five part-time employees in planting, trimming, mowing, and getting ready for harvest. "It's a family business," says Taylor, "my dad has been in it for forty years. He still works part time helping with the maintenance of the equipment."

In larger plantations there may be ten to twenty-five full time employees with as many as several hundred part-time workers. Some of them have comprehensive managerial structures to perform production, marketing, financial, and personnel functions. Many are still a family business with family members playing major roles.

Except for managers and specialists in such fields as agronomy, horticulture, forestry, and computer technology, most workers are trained on the job. Planting, shearing, spraying, tagging, and cutting are best learned by doing them with guidance from an experienced person. Some part-time work translates into summer jobs for high school and college students.

In the peak selling season, the Warren Plantation in Kansas employs 50 to 55 people most of whom are high school kids. At Jack and Janie Scott's Merry Christmas Tree Farm in Texas, high school students work every year and when they go off to college they ask for jobs during their holidays. Other workers are people in

A sorting and loading yard at the Noble Tree Farm in Salem, Oregon.

the community who need extra money. Migratory workers come from distant places, sometimes from abroad, and stay in housing that is provided. All work for money, but the out-of-doors has a special attraction. The wonderful world of Christmas trees is a wonderful place to work!

Some jobs such as the spraying for insects are frequently contracted with firms that provide pilots and airplanes. Helicopters and trucks are also acquired in this way. Extensive use is made of computer technology in accounting and finance, and scheduling a large variety of operations. When trucks depart to deliver trees to wholesale and retail customers, computers often monitor the entire process. A telephone call will tell the customer the location of the truck with his trees on a real time basis.

Approximately half the growers market trees in only one state with the remainder selling in two or more. A few market trees in many parts of the world. Every city of any size has independent lot operators

as well as civic fund raising groups such as the Scouts and Kiwanis. Nurseries and garden centers account for a considerable number as do chain stores or mass merchandisers such as Wal-Mart. Twenty-five percent of the trees are sold by farms where people can choose and cut their trees.

Thirty-five Million Real Christmas Trees

Seventy-two percent of all American households have a Christmas tree of some type with somewhat more than a half reporting an artificial tree. The number of real trees sold has totaled about 35 million for the United States, Canada and Mexico. During the past forty years imports from Canada have dropped significantly, primarily because most trees now come from plantations not the northern forests. Customers can select from a large variety of shapes, sizes and kinds of trees with prices ranging from $10 to $40 with an average price of $25.

Christmas Tree Species in North America

Many species of Christmas trees flourish in North America. The growing areas of the most popular ones are indicated in the map on page 47. These trees are shown in color photographs on the two pages that follow with a listing of other species on page 87. Quite a number are grown in regions in which they are not indigenous. A few are more limited, such as the Noble fir, which grows well only in the Northwest of the United States.

The popularity of particular kinds of trees has varied over the years. In 1948, the top five were Balsam fir, Douglas fir, Black spruce, Eastern red cedar, and White spruce. In 1955, Douglas fir took first place followed by a newcomer, Scotch pine, which moved to fifth place. The two spruces had dropped out of the top five. Scotch pine took the lead a few years later only to be followed by Douglas fir and Balsam fir.

Particular trees are popular for many reasons. Availability is important. The northeast has always had a plentiful supply of Balsam fir trees from Maine and Nova Scotia. In Pennsylvania and beyond, Scotch pine became the most popular tree only to be challenged a few years later by Douglas fir. In North Carolina and adjoining states, Fraser firs have become favorites and in the west, Douglas firs retain a strong lead.

Regional differences continue to be important but less so as improved technology and transportation make a larger variety of trees available everywhere.

Post-season Christmas trees ready for recycling.
Courtesy National Christmas Tree Association

Plantations play a major role in giving people a greater variety of species from which to choose. Shipment by truck and scheduling by computer help bring trees from more distant places. The wider range of choices and active promotion by growers influence the kinds of trees that people buy. There are other reasons for picking a particular tree.

A grandmother in New York with a German heritage commented, "we choose a Balsam fir with branches far apart so we can light our tree with candles." "My father and mother liked Scotch pine and so do we," said an Ohio woman. A college student in British Columbia, "I go out and cut a Douglas fir in the nearby forest, I think that is what it is called. Whatever, so long as it's not an artificial tree. I like the smell of evergreen." Norma from Asheville, North Carolina, said, "We always pick the tallest Fraser fir we can possibly put into our living room. Last year we had to cut a lot off the bottom to make it fit." Jane in Macomb, Illinois, reports, "I didn't like the tree my husband picked, a few too many martinis I think. Next year I am going to do it."

Christmas Trees Are Environmentally Friendly

Evergreen trees provide benefits beyond the beauty they offer at Christmas time. In the words of Keith Jacobs, "Christmas trees create scenic green belts, stabilize soil, protect water supplies, and provide refuge for wildlife." Passing motorists can view beautiful Christmas trees all year long. They even breath a little easier with the oxygen created by the trees. Each acre of trees produces the daily oxygen requirements for eighteen people.

After the Christmas season many caring souls move their trees into the garden to become bird shelters and feeders. Trees are sunk into ponds or lakes to make refuge and feeding areas for fish. Erosion control, composting, and fuel are other post-holiday uses. Probably the most important benefit of recycled trees is the mulch and soil enrichment they provide for gardens, parks, and farms.

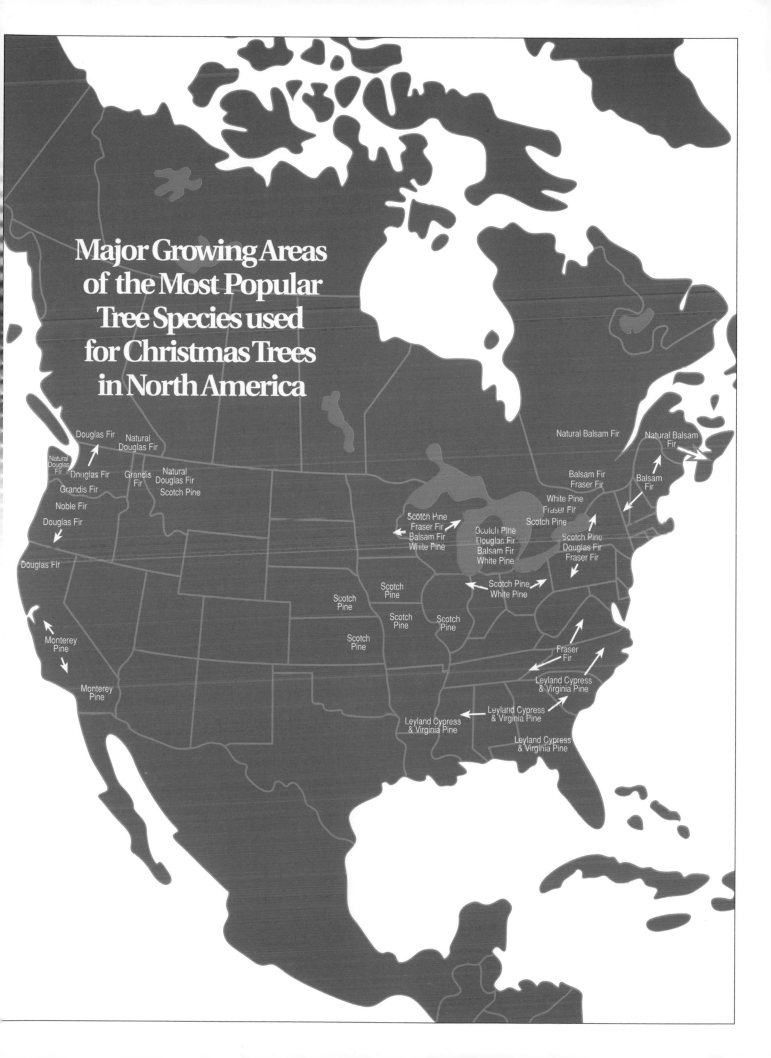

Major Growing Areas of the Most Popular Tree Species used for Christmas Trees in North America

POPULAR CHRISTMAS TREE

Douglas Fir

Natural Douglas Fir

Noble Fir

Scotch Pine

Grandis Fir

Leyland Cypress

SPECIES IN NORTH AMERICA

Monterey Pine

Balsam Fir

White Pine

Virginia Pine

Natural Balsam Fir

Fraser Fir

Christmas tree fence at Port Fourchon, Lafourche Parish, Louisiana, to help restore coastal marshes. Thousands of trees are used to enhance sedimentation and prevent salt water intrusion. Courtesy Clarke J. Gernon, Sr

Christmas Trees Create Dunes in Texas

Galveston Island on the Texas gulf coast found a special use for Christmas trees after a hurricane destroyed a major part of its dune system. Dunes form from the bottom up and require a strong root structure. After a great deal of experimentation, it was found that discarded Christmas trees laid horizontally and stacked in rows provide an effective base for the creation of dunes. A similar technique is used in Louisiana to restore its coastal marshes. Thousands of trees are placed in fenced areas to block salt water intrusion and enhance sedimentation.

Recycling Christmas Trees in St. Louis and San Diego

In St. Louis and adjoining areas, public and private groups sponsor a massive recycling program for Christmas trees.[11] The day after Christmas a publicity program goes into full swing. With the headline, "Give a Gift to the Environment, Recycle Your Christmas Tree!", the St. Louis Post-Dispatch prints a long list of collection sites. Posters appear everywhere, radio commercials add their bit, and telephone calls help close the gap. Most of the trees are chipped into mulch that is available at various centers without

cost. Others create wildlife habitats and fish beds.

Within a period of ten years, San Diego, California, experienced a sixfold increase in the number of recycled trees. Between December 27 and January 17, people deliver their trees to twenty-eight convenient centers, such as parks, schools, shopping centers, and tree nurseries in their effort to be environmentally friendly.

Artificial Trees End Up in Landfills

In Wauwatosa, Wisconsin, a suburb of Milwaukee, Christmas trees are collected for recycling during a one week period early in January.[12] People are informed about time and place through announcements in city newsletters. City employees and trucks collect the trees. Wauwatosa discovered that Christmas tree mulch was highly useful and cost effective in landscaping and planting. Howard Young, the Engineering & Operations Administrator, evaluated the program, "What we have done has been very positive. We average 81 tons of recycled Christmas trees per year. You can't do that with those plastic bottle brushes they call artificial trees. They can't be recycled and just end up in the landfills."

Workers in Wauwatosa, Wisconsin in process of mulching the community's Christmas trees. Courtesy National Christmas Tree Association

Picking up the mulch.
Courtesy National Christmas Tree Association

Taking Home the Mulch After Christmas

The city forestry department of Fort Dodge, Iowa, sets up a shredder in a park early in January to mulch Christmas trees. This service is free to people who take their trees to the park. For those who prefer, a local club will pick up trees at the curb for a small fee. Fran Long, the owner of a choose and cut farm, reports that "it is kind of strange, but many people get a kick out of seeing their Christmas tree get 'eaten' by the shredder." Some of them "will bring a bag with them, and take the mulch from their trees home with them"[13]

Millions of Trees are Recycled

Recycling Christmas trees has become a major project throughout North America. A recent survey of twenty-five of the largest cities in the United States indicated that more than one half of a total of four million trees had been recycled.[14] Equally impressive results have been ob- tained in other cities and communities. The number of recycled trees has increased by many millions in recent years and the future holds even greater prospects. Economic and environmental benefits have combined to give people a rationale for recycling.

Choose and Cut Christmas Tree Farms

In rural America of the past, the joy of Christmas for many families began with a trip to the woods to search for the perfect Christmas tree. The Noël Christmas Tree Farm of Santa Barbara, California, reminds people, "You can relive those days again by walking through our 'forest' and choose and cut your own tree." More than 5,000 tree farms offer such an experience. Most of them came into existence less than 20 years ago, and to repeat the words of Fred Strathmeyer, Sr., "The choose and cut idea has taken off nationwide like gangbusters."

Some choose and cut farms are a part-time pursuit. The largest farms have 500 acres of trees, but two-thirds of them have less than 25 acres. Most sell from 500 to 1,000 trees a year. They sell more than Christmas trees.

Where Christmas Memories Begin

Bob Scott's Prairie Pines Christmas Tree Farm a mile outside Wichita, Kansas, is "Where Christmas Memories Begin." Eighty acres of trees and a chalet style barn create a special ambience for families who come to cut their trees. Professional carolers, horse-

Christmas at Prairie Pines, Wichita, Kansas.

drawn wagons, hot chocolate and wassail, and a visit from Santa Claus add to the aura of an "old-fashioned Christmas." The rustic barn with its massive fireplace has become a popular setting for Christmas parties and for meetings and weddings all year.

Christmas Trees, Gourmet Breakfast, and a Dog Named Simon

Homesteaded in the late 1880's, a pine country farm near the town of Pearl River, Louisiana, gained notoriety in 1925 when it was sold to Norma Badon, the infamous "madam" in the French Quarter of New Orleans. For twenty years the farm was a retreat and summer home for "her and the girls." After that it served a more mundane function as an airstrip until purchased in 1955 by the Gernon family.

The Shady Pond Tree Farm, as it is known today, is owned by Clarke Gernon, Sr. who grows sixteen thousand Christmas trees on the forty-five acres of land. Oak and magnolia trees line the drive leading to row upon row of exotic conifers, a scene that is highlighted in January and February by two hundred varieties of blooming camellias.

With an advanced degree in engineering, Clarke J. Gernon, Sr. is credited with literally scores of innovations. He is active in community projects and professional associations. His biography appears in all of the major *Who's* Who' in the United States and abroad. All of this does not mean that Gernon has not experienced difficult times.

During a bleak winter day almost ten years ago, the "blues" set in as Gernon surveyed the results of his Christmas tree sales. Fewer customers had shown up and sales had dropped to new lows. Gernon described his mood, "Supper, that cold December evening, was taken in near total silence. Having had little experience with defeat, I had no desire to learn. The course of action was clear. Shady Pond Tree Farm had to be recreated."[15]

An inspiration came quite suddenly. Shady Pond Tree Farm was going to become an 'exotic Christmas tree plantation'. Gernon headed for his study and gathered every planting stock catalog he could find and listed exotic trees. Among them were various strains of Leyland cypress, Sitka spruce, Japanese black pine, and Deodar cedar. Orders were placed the next morning and every tree on Gernon's list was acquired except one.

Customers have responded positively and now return each season to see what is new. The media have joined to feature the display of exotic trees with the local NBC affiliate broadcasting a morning show from the farm.

Like Marmaduke of comic strip fame, the Shady Pond Tree Farm has Simon, a Labrador with similar propensities. Simon follows the equipment in the fields catching the sticks that fly out from under the cutters until he has six to eight in his mouth. At other times he spends his time chasing insects. Visiting children like to watch Simon and give him toys and gifts.

During one moonless night, Clarke Gernon was preparing the machines for the next day when he heard what sounded like animal feet approaching the old barn. There in the distance was a deer, but the shortest deer he had ever seen. It was Simon carrying a skull plate with antlers in his mouth!

Dining on a gourmet breakfast in the mansion on Gernon's exotic Christmas tree farm is more than a little out of the ordinary. Two of Louisiana's renowned chefs, Chef John Folse from Lafitt's Landing and Chef Michael Roussel from Brennan's are there to prepare the food. Menus feature outstanding cuisine of the region, such as Creole corn and shrimp soup, crawfish scrambled eggs, Andouille with grits, and eggs Hussarde, a blend of exotic food in the midst of exotic Christmas trees.

Shady Pond Tree Farm, Denham Springs, Louisiana.

Christmas Trees, a Wildlife Sanctuary, and Maple Syrup

In 1969, the Baxter family purchased a thirty-two acre hayfield on the top of a mountain in Afton, New York, as a country retreat. Since then their expanse of country living has grown to include four ponds stocked with fish, a wildlife sanctuary for deer, turkeys, birds, a bear with her cub, a stand of maple trees for syrup, two large greenhouses, and a quarter million conifer trees.

Bruce and Charlotte Baxter.

At Christmas time, the Baxters don't just sell Christmas trees, they invite families to visit the farm to create a Christmas memory. Charlotte Baxter writes, "We want entire families (including pets) to come to the farm and wander through our wonderland of trees, take pictures and make a Christmas memory. It's usually very cold and snowy during the Christmas season, so we always have a fire in the old cast-iron stove and hot apple cider, hot chocolate and cookies at no charge to our guests. We have a few sleds to lend to guests with small children. It's tough to look for a tree while carrying a tot."

The Baxters have many fond memories of people from Christmases past. One very cold and snowy morning a man wandered off to "find a perfect tree." Late in the day his car was still in the parking lot. The Baxters thought he might be lost or hurt so they began to look for him. They found him with a tree he had cut hours before and enjoying the scenery.

On one rainy afternoon, a husband, wife, and young daughter arrived with a large umbrella and anxious to find their tree. After some time had passed father and daughter came in to get warm. Several hours later and no wife. The husband said it was quite normal for his wife to take a long time to find a tree. Finally, she arrived to rest and then wanted to search again. The husband said, "Honey, stay here and get warm. I'll be back in a minute." He came back in five minutes with a tree —she loved it! They have returned every year since.

A strange request had come a few years earlier when a full moon was to coincide with a couple's anniversary. For a reason known only to them, the husband and wife wanted to cut their tree on the stroke of midnight. The Baxters were told not to wait up for them. Prepayment was not offered but the couple left their money in the "honor box."

Tree farming is truly a labor of love. Bruce Baxter is out almost every day in all kinds of weather doing most of the work, mowing, spraying, and shearing, alone. In 1996 he received recognition as the Outstanding Tree Farmer in the State of New York.

A Second Life Among the Trees

For Jack and Janie Scott of Tomball, Texas, the Merry Christmas Tree Farm began as a "retirement project" but soon became a full-time pursuit. They describe what they call their 'second life' in this way, "We can't think of anything else we'd rather do. To see the excitement on the faces of the children as they climb on the wagons with saws and

Children's tour of the Merry Christmas Tree Farm, Tomball, Texas.

measuring sticks, and the fun the family members have together as they pick out the tree that is just right for them, is a great pleasure." There are daytime tours for children, night time hayride parties for church and school groups, a farm animal petting zoo with a pot bellied pig, and a visit from Santa Claus on weekends. A great way to begin the Christmas season.

A Legacy of the Dust Bowl Years

The Williams Tree Farm, Rockton, Illinois, began as a dairy farm in the early 1940's in an area known as 'sand prairie'. To keep their sandy soil from blowing away, the Williams joined the government conservation program and planted evergreen trees as a barrier. This legacy from the dust bowl years of the thirties spawned a new business a few years later. The Williams began to cut their trees to profit from a shortage of Christmas trees. They planted sixty thousand trees the next year, most of which died. If at first you don't succeed, try try again, the Williams thought, and planted another fifty thousand. Forty years and four generations later the original dairy farm has become a Christmas tree farm of 350 acres.[16] Another 140 acres are set aside as wetlands and wildlife habitat, and the remainder for other crops.

More than a producer of Christmas trees, the farm offers a "people centered event" which has become an important part of the holiday celebration for many. In the words of Karen Williams, "We try to create an atmosphere of wonder and celebration." So they do! Families can take a horse-drawn hayride or a trolley-train ride through the maze of trees to find their special tree. There is a scenic covered bridge, a children's farm with reindeer, fox, goats, and sheep, a large barn, a gift shop, and a snack shop called the Candy Cane Cafe.

A Special Curriculum for School Children

Larry and Jackie Cavaletto, who own the Noël Christmas Tree Farm, Santa Barbara, California, offer an educational farm tour for school children. All the steps of growing Christmas trees are covered, the planting of the seed from pine cones, transplanting into fields, the cultivation and care of the trees, and finally the cutting and selling. After the talk the children climb aboard the farm train for a ride to see trees at various stages of growth. Special packets are available for teachers and videos can be borrowed. Every child is given a coloring book and a chance to win a coloring contest.

The Noël Tree Farm has a life-sized nativity scene with live animals to show the real meaning of Christmas. More fun at a haystack play area with bales of hay arranged as a fort with tunnels and crawl spaces along with loose hay to jump in. Ample parking spaces and picnic tables for lunch or snacks are provided. Families bring cameras and camcorders to capture the memories of the day.

A wagon ride at the Williams Tree Farm, Rockton, Illinois.

Joe Montana Buys His Christmas Tree

Dwayne Dale's Sports Center Christmas Tree Farm in Topeka, Kansas, has a nine-hole golf course, three miniature golf courses, a golf driving range, a baseball batting facility, and volleyball courts. Peg Kirby of the Kirby Tree Farm in Toddville, Iowa, stores 150 dozen cookies in her freezer and has twenty-one gallon bags of instant cocoa ready for hot water awaiting the arrival of customers. Steve and Fran Hendricks of Weleetka, Oklahoma, give a free snapshot with every tree purchased. Buzz and Janet Warren's tree farm in Stanley, Kansas, features a Christmas egg hunt for little children and claims Joe Montana, the football star, as a customer.

A fun train at the Noël Christmas Tree Farm, Santa Barbara, California.

cold weather can add misery and discomfort. Too much for Karl Litzinger. For several years now Karl has ordered his Christmas tree from the Land O'Pines Nursery, located in Custer, Michigan. The perfect tree arrives at the front door packed in a box at the right time for Christmas. It was cut within forty-eight hours of shipment and packaged in a plastic bag for later disposal.[19] A sturdy stand that holds five quarts of water to keep the tree fresh is available. Nothing like the aroma of a real tree.

Choose and Cut in Mexico

In Mexico, the crèche has been more important as a Christmas symbol than the tree. Indeed, there was considerable opposition to Christmas trees from the Mexican government. A few companies such as the Kirk Company and the J. Hofert Company exported a modest number of trees to Mexico prior of the eighties. In subsequent years the number has gradually increased to well over a million trees today.[17] Approximately three hundred thousand are produced in Mexico, a few are wild trees but most are grown on plantations.

One of the largest plantations is located on the edge of Mexico City with more than six hundred thousand trees.[18] Twenty-five thousand trees are sold each year to customers who choose and cut their own trees with the two thousand hand saws made available to them. There are ten miles of roadways and a parking area for three thousand cars. The owner, Ernesto S. Maurer, maintains a petting zoo of ninety animals, including deer and pygmy pigs, and a bazaar that features local handicraft and candy. He has a flock of 350 sheep on his plantation to do the weeding, but if the number is not limited they nibble on the trees.

Sitting It Out

Not everyone takes a trip to a choose and cut farm or even the corner lot a few blocks away. Snow, ice, and

Christmas Tree Farming in Europe

A rough estimate is that somewhere around sixty million Christmas trees were displayed in Europe during recent years.[20] Give or take a few million! Relatively few are artificial trees but the number is uncertain and differs from country to country. The European growers association estimates that fifty-two million trees are harvested annually in Europe with sales of about fifty million. Much of these data lack the advantage of scientific surveys and do not always agree with other sources.[21]

Many European trees, especially those grown in Germany and such northern countries as Norway and Finland, come from forests but the number of plantations has increased in recent years. Most trees are not as extensively sheared or trimmed as they are in North America. The traditional tree with considerable space between the branches is still preferred. Some people light their trees with candles, but the hazards of fire have greatly reduced the number.

The environmental compatibility of the natural product is a major consideration.[22] Recycling has become an important pursuit in many European cities and communities. Some European countries have organized Christmas tree growers associations and a European association has also been established.

Christmas trees in front of the two-hundred year old farm house of Helferts Hof in Odenwald located near Heidelberg, Germany.

Selling trees in the farmyard of Helferts Hof.

Shropshire sheep used for weed control at Helferts Hof.

Christmas Trees in Germany

In Germany where Christmas trees originated, the number of trees displayed has been estimated to be between 22 to 23 million trees which is equivalent to the United States on a per capita basis.[23] The number of artificial trees is low but has increased in recent years.

Spruce and fir trees, many of which come from the Black Forest, Bavarian Forests, and Thuringer Forests are the most popular.[24] Somewhat over three million trees are imported, primarily from Denmark. The demand for the more exotic species, such as the Nordmann fir, the Noble fir, Grand fir, and Korean fir has expanded.

The number of trees grown on plantations has increased significantly in recent years with techniques and equipment similar to those in North America. A major difference is that the trees are not normally sheared to promote density. Fifty percent of German trees are sold in flower shops and garden centers, 35 percent in Christmas tree markets, and 15 percent come directly from the forests.

Helferts Hof, a German Tree Plantation

Most German tree plantations are full-time enterprises. An exception is that of Raimund Kohl who started growing Christmas trees on a part-time basis in 1968. Kohl's farm called Helferts Hof has been in the family since the 16th century. He produces his own seedlings and transplants which are planted with a hand hoe on the steep slopes of the farm. The gaps that result from cutting are continually planted with new trees. Shropshire sheep, a special strain from Scotland, are used for weed management and they have not damaged any of the trees![25] Three thousand trees are sold each year directly at the farm to consumers who come from the nearby cities of Mannheim and Heidelberg. The price per foot ranges from three DM's or two dollars for the least expensive trees, six DM's or four dollars for medium priced trees, and up to ten DM's or six dollars for the best trees. Five to ten percent of Kohl's trees are sold to people who choose and cut.

Denmark at the Center of the Stage

Denmark is a small country that plays a big role as the largest exporter of Christmas trees and greenery in Europe.[26] Most of the Danish production of between five and six million trees goes for export to a long list of European countries, including many formerly behind the Communist iron curtain. Approximately one and a half million trees are sold within Denmark.[27] The few artificial trees are found in public places such as stores and hotels.

In addition to state-owned and private forests, many Christmas trees come from land categorized as farmland. Trees are sold through forest rangers, foreign and domestic wholesalers, and an array of local retail outlets.

The Langesø estate in Denmark, which contains more than 2200 acres of Christmas trees and forest, is the site of an annual fair for the Christmas tree industry in Europe and elsewhere. Courtesy Finn Jacobsen, Skovrider, Langesø Skovbrug

The Nordmann fir has played a major part in Danish exports. This aristocrat of Christmas trees was introduced to Denmark in the middle of the last century from the mountainous regions of the eastern end of the Black Sea and has been constantly improved through the years. Europeans pay a premium price for these quality trees. Some Nordmann firs are slightly trimmed to give them a bit of density for people who light with electricity. A more traditional tree is available for those who still prefer candles.

Since 1992, Denmark has sponsored an annual Fair attended by two thousand Christmas tree growers, buyers, and suppliers from Europe and elsewhere. The Fair is held at the Langesø estate in August with the goal of keeping participants informed about recent developments. Langesø was privately owned until 1977, most recently by the Holsten family, which donated it as a center for Danish forest research and development. Large expanses of forests and Christmas trees surround the main buildings of the 2,200 acre estate.

Nordmann fir. Courtesy Jøn Dalum

The British Christmas Tree Industry

In 1848 when Queen Victoria and her family gathered around their tree at Windsor Castle, Christmas trees in Britain were the exception rather than the rule. Today, the British grow four and one-half million Christmas trees a year and import an additional five hundred thousand trees mostly from Denmark and the Benelux countries.[28]

The Norway spruce is the most popular tree with about sixty percent of the market. Such exotic trees as the Nordmann and Noble fir have captured a sizable following as have Scots and Lodgepole pines. British growers like those in North America are constantly seeking ways to improve the quality of their trees.

A few of the British growers are large. For example, the Yattendon Estates in Berkshire has a total population of more than a million trees. Most growers are relatively small and produce fewer than five thousand trees a year. Local labor is employed for cultivating, shearing, and harvesting and most trees are sold by supermarkets, garden centers, and farm stores. People also buy trees from greengrocers and flower shops and there are always a few 'wheeler-dealers'. Some tree growers sell directly through their own markets and there is an increase in the number of choose and cut farms.

Although prices differ in various localities, most of the smaller trees sell for £10 to £15 or about $16 to $24; large trees for business, schools, and public buildings may cost £200 or $360 and more. For people who prefer not to pay, tree rustling has become a major pursuit. Security measures, such as sophisticated alarm systems, guard dog patrols, geese, and trip wires have become increasingly necessary.

Christmas trees and a traditional Danish mill. Photographed by Soren Fodgaard, courtesy Jøn Dalum, Danish Christmas Tree Producers Association

Real Trees in France

Approximately 5.6 million households or 25 percent of the total households in France purchase real Christmas trees.[29] The total in number of trees is 5.8 million with an estimated value of some 423 million francs. The number can vary significantly from year to year as evidenced by a drop of 12.5 percent in a recent year. Most are grown on French farms or plantations with about 15 percent coming from Belgium and Denmark. Norway spruce has the greatest share of the market with Nordmann firs coming in second. Seventy percent of the trees are cut with the remainder grown in pots.

Scandinavian and Benelux Countries

In the northern countries of Norway, Sweden, and Finland, 95 percent of a total of about four million trees are real trees, most of which come from the forests.[30] The Benelux countries have a thriving Christmas tree industry which produces four million trees for local households and another two million for export. The percentage of households buying trees in Austria is about the same as for Germany. Switzerland harvests about a million trees and imports another half million. Fewer Swiss households have trees than those in Austria or Germany, partly because 30 percent have a French and Italian cultural heritage.

Iceland and Ireland

From ten to twelve thousand trees are grown in Iceland, mostly pine and Norway spruce, and an additional twenty two thousand are imported from Denmark.[31] It takes fifteen to eighteen years to grow a six-foot tree, more than twice the average time required in the United States. The four hundred thousand trees grown in Ireland come from plantations and forests that did not exist before 1904 when the government began a forestation project.[32] A quarter of these are exported which means that only about 30 percent of Irish homes have Christmas trees. Ireland plans to increase its production to a million trees by the year 2,000 and compete with such major exporters as Denmark and Benelux countries.

Southern Europe

The number of trees sold annually in Italy, Spain, and Portugal has been estimated to total 2.5 million with a harvest of one million.[33] These estimates could be far too low in the light of reports that several million trees are grown in Italy alone. Although this number may well be too high, the production of trees in Italy has increased significantly in recent years. In all of the southern countries a large percentage of trees are imported from the northern countries. Artificial trees are also found in great abundance.

New Year Trees in Russia

A relatively low number of trees is harvested and sold in the former communistic eastern European countries. Based on an estimate of eight million trees by the European growers association, about seven or eight percent of the households have trees. Most of the Russian trees are New Year rather than Christmas trees. In Moscow, more than a hundred markets, generally located near metro stations, begin selling real trees in mid-December. St. Petersburg has a large central market at Sennaya Ploshchad with smaller markets in other parts of the city. Sizable markets for real trees are found the Baltic countries, Poland, the Czech Republic, and Hungary. The number of Christmas and New Year trees that are grown and sold in the former communist countries will undoubtedly increase significantly with expanded economic development. Many of the Russian New Year trees are likely to become Christmas trees or at least serve a double purpose.

CHRISTMAS TREES IN GLAMOROUS ATTIRE

The beauty of a Christmas tree is truly in the eyes of the beholder. An elderly lady was seen sitting in front of a small badly-shaped tree with a few branches and only four candles. Not much of a tree, but the expression on her face showed otherwise. Christmas trees create happy faces on children and adults alike. Each tree is endowed with a magic touch that transcends its material being.

Christmas trees become more magnificent through the settings that surround them. Rooms in mansions are themselves the masterful creations of architects and interior designers. A special enchantment comes from interesting and unique places. First Ladies bestow a political veneer as they seek to create more beautiful and memorable trees. Family and community traditions and the heritage of history give trees a special meaning.

At Home for Christmas

Christmas at the Vanden Bergs

A short distance from the town square of Pella, Iowa, is the home of Jim and Jan Vanden Berg. In walking up to the front door on a moonlit night, visitors are met with an array of holiday displays and lights to introduce the attractions that are found within. The front door opens to a wide hall and balustraded staircase

The Vanden Berg home reflected in moonlight and Christmas decor.

bedecked with white ribbons, fabric roses, and dark green pine boughs. To the left is the formal parlor with white furniture and a Christmas tree trimmed in white ribbons and large silk roses which repeat the rose motif on the dark green border of the wallcovering. To the right is the great room with the largest tree in the home. The ornaments on the tree in this casual setting are made of burgundy and hunter green quilted fabrics and antique buttons. The Vanden Berg trees were decorated by the Pella Garden Club and the house opened to the public for the annual Pella Christmas Tour of Homes.

Christmas trees have always played an important part in the Vanden Berg celebration of Christmas. Jan describes their very first tree as one of a kind "Charley Brown Christmas Tree," which Jim, her husband of two weeks, found on a friend's farm during a blizzard. Dragging the rather hefty tree up the stairways to their then third floor apartment was not an easy task. Where to put it was a problem as Jan commented, "We were lucky we had a big corner to put it in."

During later years three Vanden Berg children, Jenni, John, and Jessica joined the annual search for a perfect tree. Dad would put it in the stand and string the lights, and the whole family help deck it with special ornaments. The task wasn't complete until hand-made ornaments, grandma's hand crocheted Christmas balls, tatted snowflakes, garlands, and a shining star were in place.

Christmas begins early for people with a Dutch heritage. At the Vanden Berg home, Sinter Klaas arrives late at night on December 6 to bring gifts for the children. This tradition dates back to Saint Nicholas, a charitable and kindly Bishop in the fourth century, who was the inspiration for the mythical character identified as Sinter Klaas in Dutch and Santa Claus in English. Before bedtime wooden shoes are put out by the children and somehow the next morning they contain chocolate candy, Dutch mints, and spice cookies. Jan's homemade Dutch letters, a delicious almond filling in a crust shaped like the letter S, and almond coffee cake make breakfast a special treat, a preview for the regular Christmas season.

Christmas tree trimmed with white ribbons and large silk roses.

Christmas tree with ornaments of burgundy and hunter green quilted fabrics and antique buttons.

On Christmas Eve the Vanden Bergs attend a candlelight service in their church. Back home the children open one gift and before bedtime put cookies and milk out for Santa Claus. Christmas morning they have to find the stockings that Santa always hides after which the family exchanges gifts. In the evening the Vanden Berg family and friends share in good food and wonderful stories. Son John and wife Shari, who live in a nearby city, come with their young son Carter. Jan expresses their feelings about their first grandson, "What fun he is to have at Christmas!"

The extended Vanden Berg family includes John and Jessica, standing, seated in rear from left to right, Shari, Jim, and Jenni, in front is Jan holding grandson, Carter.

Christmas at Hamilton Field, 1935. Courtesy Ruth Reid

Christmas Past at Hamilton Field

Colonel Walter Hough's career spanned two world wars. He earned his wings in flimsy World War I airplanes which required courage merely to fly. Too old for combat missions in World War II, his expertise in communications made an important contribution to the war effort. A major in 1935, Hough and his wife, Marion, a former army nurse, are shown with their Christmas tree at Hamilton Field near San Francisco. After he left the service at age 60 in 1948, the Houghs spent their retirement years in Washington, D.C. They are both buried in Arlington National Cemetery.

The Ehlers in Berlin

Jan Otto and Gisela Ehlers and their three children, Kristian, Jacob, and Karsten, live in a three-story house in the Wannsee section of Berlin. They originally came from the small town of Bredstedt near the Danish border in the state of Schleswig Holstein. Christmas Eve at the Ehlers family home was a special occasion as family and friends gathered for a dinner of smoked eel, lamb, boiled potatoes, and rote Grütze. To whet the appetite, Jan Otto's mother, Katrine, traditionally serves a bit of cheer with her own potent blend of brandy and fruit that has fermented for several weeks.

The Ehlers Christmas tree in Berlin.

After he completed his studies at the Universities of Freiberg and Kiel, Jan Otto holds an administrative position with the German Social Security Administration. For the past twenty-three years he has commuted more than sixty kilometers by automobile through the crowded thoroughfares of Berlin to his office. Gisela splits her daytime hours between a nearby Kindergarten and home.

Life became more hectic for the Ehlers after the fall of the infamous Berlin Wall in 1989 and the choice of Berlin as the capital of a united Germany. Massive construction projects are remaking the city, especially the Potsdamer Platz at the center which has been a large vacant landscape since the end of the war. Beneath all of this land is the bunker in which Hitler spent his last days before he committed suicide.

The Ehlers Christmas tree is a traditional tree which appears on the morning of December 24 ready for the family festivities on Christmas Eve. The whole family and especially the children are enthralled with the fragrance of the tree and the light cast by the candles. Three or four days after the new year begins the tree is removed to be replaced the next year by another beautiful tree.

Yes, There is a Santa Claus!

Keith and Norma Colton live in Cedar Rapids, Iowa, with their three children, Kimberly, Jeffrey, and Benjamin. Keith is the sales manager for an automobile dealership and Norma, in her own words, is "very happy being a full-time homemaker."

The Christmas season for the Coltons begins with a trip to the Hoffman Tree Farm the first weekend after Thanksgiving to choose their tree. After much joyful chatter, the ornaments which had been stored in the closet since the last Christmas somehow find their rightful place on the tree. It has become a tradition to add an ornament every year for Kimberly, Jeffrey, and Benjamin. Each ornament is marked with the year and the age of the

child. To give emphasis to the true meaning of Christmas a lighted nativity scene is placed near the tree.

Christmas Eve begins with a special family dinner in sight of the tree after which the Coltons attend church services. When they return home the children search for a pickle ornament hidden on the tree. The one who finds it gets to open the first package. Some of the gifts are left for Christmas morning and others for exchanges with grandparents and friends.

A few years earlier the children had decided that there really wasn't a Santa Claus. After the Christmas Eve dinner that year, Keith loaded the children into the car for church and waited several minutes for Norma to come out of the house. After the church services the children were told that a note had been left for Santa asking him to stop earlier than usual. The children laughed at this big joke. When the family arrived home gifts had appeared under the tree with a note from Santa. The children were more than a little amazed and agreed that there must be a Santa after all.

Trees With Straw Decorations

Families in Finland traditionally decorate their trees with national flags and straw ornaments for display on Christmas Eve. At sunset they make their way to the churchyard to pay homage to the graves of loved ones. They return home where the children anxiously await the visit of Father Christmas who comes in person with a basket of presents and asks: "Are there any good children

The Colton family and Christmas tree, from left to right, Benjamin, Jeffrey, Kimberly, and parents Norma and Keith.

Finnish mother and children decorating tree with straw ornaments.

here?" "Yes," say the children to this man, who is usually their father, a relative, or a family friend. The children sing a song or two to Father Christmas who tells them about his long trip from Lapland, the northern land with many reindeer. They then sit down for the main Christmas meal with favorite family dishes and a dessert of rice pudding hiding an almond. Luck for the whole year goes to the one whose dessert contains the prize. Lively conversation make it a truly joyous occasion for all, including any children and grandchildren from afar.

Christmas Day is more of an anticlimax in Finland. The morning often begins with church services, but for the most part the day is quietly spent with family and friends. The following day is another holiday, St. Stephen's Day, and New Year's Eve invites more celebration. It all ends on Epiphany, the sixth of January.

In Worldwide Views

The Tree That Sailed for Christmas

The fifty foot tree cut in a forest overlooking snow-capped mountains in the Pacific Northwest was moved by truck to Portland, Oregon, where it was loaded on a Matson line ship for the long sea journey to sunny Hawaii. Upon arrival the tree was transported to the front of Honolulu Hale, the city hall, and beautifully decorated for Christmas. In what has become an annual tradition, families from all parts of the island come there to enjoy the giant barefoot "Shaka" Santa and the lavish holiday displays. A special treat was the tree that sailed all the way from the mainland for a place among the palms.

A Christmas tree among the palms. Photographed by David Franzen, courtesy Alexander & Baldwin

Christmas tree in lobby of Atlantic Hotel, Hamburg, Germany.

The Man Behind the Paneling

The Atlantic Hotel in Hamburg, Germany, has housed literally hundreds of famous people since it was founded in 1909. Emperor Hirohito of Japan, and Edward, the Prince of Wales, were welcomed together with such rich commoners as Henry Ford, and J. P. Morgan. The King of Siam brought his own chefs and twelve pages. More recently the names of Boris Yeltsin, Whoopi Goldberg, Jane Fonda, and Michael Jackson appeared on the registry.

During the fire bombing of Hamburg in World War II, the hotel building remained virtually intact. The menu recognized the possibility of air raids by noting that "our guests are requested to pay immediately." The English seized the hotel in 1945 and used it as officers quarters for five years.

At Christmas time a tree stands in the lobby where a large portrait of Emperor Wilhelm II can also be seen. The painting was found behind paneling during restoration work in 1979, uncovered, and then for some unknown reason hidden again for another five years.

The British Ambassadors' Christmas Tree

An outstanding Christmas tree in a special setting is the one found in the ballroom of the British Embassy in Washington, D.C. It was in this room in 1991 that Queen Elizabeth II gave a banquet for President and Mrs. Bush during Her State Visit. The tree is a Fraser fir grown in West Virginia by Eric and Gloria Sundback who also provided trees in 1979, 1981, and 1987 for the Blue Room of the White House.

The tree with its myriad of lights and elegant ornamentation embellish the room as a single decorative unit. All are reflected in the mirrored wall panels set apart by adjacent pilasters. The carved frieze topping the pilasters executed in the style of the master British woodcarver, Grinling Gibbons, continues around the room and into the corridors. The three

British Ambassador's Tree, Washington D.C.
Photographed by Keith Harvey

antique chandeliers are Austrian and would have been lighted by gas in earlier times. They came from a former residence as did the great Tabriz palace carpet.

Mardi Gras tree. Courtesy Clarke J. Gernon, Sr.

The Mardi Gras Tree

Mardi Gras, the French name for Shrove Tuesday or Fat Tuesday, is the last day for merrymaking and gluttony in food and drink before forty days of abstinence that begin on Ash Wednesday. In many Catholic communities and countries, carnivals with spectacular parades, masked balls, and dancing in the street last for a week or more before Mardi Gras. Carnivals have their origin in pre-Christian pagan fertility rites related to the coming of spring and the rebirth of vegetation.

In Louisiana, some people decorate an evergreen tree at the beginning of the Mardi Gras season. When they arrive home from the parades and parties, they add to the decorations with masks and souvenirs. By the time Fat Tuesday arrives, the tree has become a beautiful display of Mardi Gras memories. Louisianian Clarke J. Gernon, Sr. adds that a real tree "is an excellent reminder that Spring is just around the corner."

The Tree That Came to College

Martin Luther may not have created the first Christmas tree, but he would have been impressed with the tree at the college that bears his name. This beautifully decorated twenty-five foot tree stands in the front lobby of the Center for Faith and Life on the campus of Luther College located in the scenic bluff country of northeast Iowa. As students and faculty pass on their way to and from class, they are rewarded with an aesthetic masterpiece that symbolizes the glorious meaning of Christmas.

Christmas tree at Luther College, Decorah, Iowa.

A Sacher Torte for Christmas

All who visit the famous Sacher Hotel in Vienna, Austria, at Christmas time will be greatly impressed with the beautiful Christmas tree in its elegant lounge. Nearby the Vienna Boys Choir sing Christmas songs in a historic chapel and the famous Lippenzaner horses perform at the Spanish Riding School. The Sacher Hotel has something that is just as well known, a cake that gave the hotel its name.

Sacher Hotel, Vienna.

Christmas tree in lobby, Sacher Hotel, Vienna.

The Sacher Torte came into being in 1832 when Prince Wenzel Clemens Metternich, one of the most influential men in Europe during the post-Napoleonic period, ordered that a new cake be prepared for his guests with the comment: "I don't want any complaints about the dessert course." The kitchen staff was understandably nervous because the *chef de cuisine* was sick. As fate would have it the responsibility finally fell to a sixteen-year old apprentice named Franz Sacher. The end result was a chocolate cake that became famous not only in Vienna but throughout the world. Sacher created a chocolate lover's dream, a cake surrounded by rich chocolate icing with more rich chocolate on the inside. Prince Metternich had no complaints from his guests, only praises for this heavenly dessert.

Sacher Torte.

In 1876, Franz Sacher's son Edvuard established his well-known delicatessen in a new building and opened guest rooms on three upper floors creating the Hotel Sacher. Edvuard died a short time later but his wife, Anna, the daughter of a Viennese butcher, took over the hotel. It was through her aplomb, ability and foresight that the Hotel Sacher became the place where the elite of Europe stayed in Vienna. Then came World War I and the fall of the Hapsburg dynasty, followed by inflation and economic disaster. In 1938 Hitler marched his army into Austria making it a part of Germany, and in 1945 Soviet troops stabled their horses in the Marble Hall, the site for so many glittering dinner parties.

The Hotel Sacher has been completely restored to its former elegance. At Christmas time after viewing the beautiful tree in the lounge, guests can add a bit of Christmas delight in the Kaffeehaus with a slice of Sacher Torte mit Slag.

Christmas tree presented by Nova Scotia to Boston as a token of gratitude for assistance given after a massive explosion in Halifax. Prudential Center Tree Lighting, Boston.

A Gift to Boston From Halifax, Nova Scotia

On December 6, 1917, a munitions ship collided with a relief ship in Halifax harbor creating one of the largest explosions of the pre-nuclear era. The blast and the tidal wave that followed flattened entire residential sections of the city. Thousands of people were killed and injured, large numbers of municipal buildings were destroyed, and services were seriously disrupted. A train from Boston was the first to arrive in Halifax with medical supplies, blankets, and building materials. Bostonians gave freely to help the cause and even the schoolchildren contributed lunch money to help the victims.

In appreciation for this generosity, Nova Scotia makes an annual gift of a Christmas tree to the people of Boston. The White spruce trees that are fifty or more feet tall come from different parts of Nova Scotia and are shipped by cargo ship or truck. A 150-foot crane is needed to lift the tree into an upright position after which scaffolding is built for the decorating. It takes 3,200 hours, 17,000 multi-colored lights, and 4.5 miles of wire to decorate the tree. A star at the top is four feet tall.

Early in December the tree lighting ceremony is held at the Prudential Center which gives special recognition to this annual gift from the appreciative people of Halifax, Nova Scotia. An array of events accompany the ceremony, including the singing of Christmas carols and a visit from Santa Claus.

Christmas at Vesterheim

The annual two-day Christmas party at the Vesterheim Norwegian-American Museum in Decorah, Iowa, is a truly festive occasion, especially for the children. The name Vesterheim came from years past when Norwegian immigrants wrote back to Norway about their western home.

More than twenty Christmas trees throughout the museum are trimmed with decorations that range from ornate Victorian ornaments to simpler paper and straw ones of the pioneer days. Norwegian food, live music, folk art and craft demonstrations, and puppet theater presentations of Christmas stories are feature attractions. Children and adults who are young at heart can have loads of fun with a variety of hands-on activities. They decorate cookies, create dolls from handkerchiefs, weave paper heart baskets, cut snowflakes from paper, and shape straw stars. The pioneers would have felt right at home.

Vesterheim Museum, Decorah, Iowa.

Christmas music at Vesterheim Museum.

Children at Christmas Festival, Vesterheim Museum

Colonial Williamsburg

During George Washington's lifetime, Williamsburg was the place to go for glamorous balls, banquets, horse races, lawn parties, theater, and politics. Although its population during that time never exceeded two thousand, Washington called it a "great metropolis" in his dairies. Between visits with Governor Dinwiddie in his Palace and meetings of the Assembly at the Capitol, Washington met with friends, played cards, drank ale and wine, and danced.

At the time Charles Minnigerode introduced the first Christmas tree in 1842, Williamsburg had already lost much of its attraction and fame as the first capital of Virginia. After the capital was moved to Richmond in 1779, Williamsburg began a rapid decline losing half of its population. By 1787, as described by John Tebbel, "all that remained was a shabby village, kept alive mostly by its farmers' market, the college, and an insane asylum."[1]

The Regency tree at the Williamsburg Inn. Courtesy Colonial Williamsburg Foundation

Through the combined vision of the Reverend Dr. W. A. R. Goodwin, former rector of the Bruton Parish Church, and John D. Rockefeller, Jr., the once shabby village of Williamsburg has regained its stature as Colonial Williamsburg.[2] What appealed especially to Rockefeller was the prospect of preserving eighty-eight of the original buildings from the 18th and early 19th centuries that "had been familiar scenes to great leaders during a critical period of our history."[3] Among them was the Bruton Parish Church which dates from 1715 and in whose churchyard many prominent people are buried.

Preservation and restoration began in 1928 with the Wren Building, the oldest academic structure in America on the campus of the second oldest college, the College of William and Mary, preceded only by Harvard. Charles Minnigerode and his friend Judge Nathaniel Beverley Tucker were both teaching there when they searched the nearby woods for a Christmas tree. The restoration continued with public structures, residences, taverns, shops, and other original Williamsburg buildings. Among them are the Public Gaol (jail), the Bruton Parish Church, Wetherburn's Tavern, a favorite of George Washington, and Market Square Tavern, the residence of Thomas Jefferson while studying law.

Christmas tree in Great Hall at Carter's Grove. Courtesy Colonial Williamsburg Foundation

Several important buildings were completely reconstructed. The most prominent of these was the Governor's Palace where Washington spent a great deal of time and Patrick Henry and Thomas Jefferson lived as governors of the commonwealth of Virginia. Another building with which all of these early Americans were intimately familiar was the Capitol that was reconstructed following the plans of the first one built in 1701-05. Sometimes referred to as the "second capitol" was Raleigh Tavern where many early Virginians assembled to consider important issues of the day.

Authentic furniture and furnishings were used to the greatest possible extent. Gardens and such other exteriors as fences and gates were included in the restorations. Within the shops, the gunsmiths, spinners and weavers, carpenters, boot and shoemakers, printers and bookbinders, wheelwrights, and harness makers conscientiously follow the techniques of the 18th century which they learned through lengthy apprenticeships.

Thirty-eight of the original buildings were residences, including the St. George Tucker House where Charles Minnigerode created a tradition that has become firmly established through the years. The Christmas trees in Colonial Williamsburg today are real trees beautifully decorated in a variety of ways. The tree that stands on a table in the Blue Room of the Tucker house shown on page 11 is much like the first one with real candles and simple decorations. A similar small tabletop tree in the Abby Aldrich Rockefeller Folk Center and shown on the cover of this book is trimmed with old toys, gilded nuts, sugar cookies, and beeswax candles. Others are much more elaborately decorated trees such as the Regency tree in the Williamsburg Inn and the tree in the Great Hall of nearby Carter's Grove.

The Christmas tree at the Williamsburg Inn is one of understated elegance and reflects the splendor of the furnishings and architectural detail of its surroundings. The handmade ornaments were especially created for this tree and are all of Regency design, a period of English artistic influence prevalent during the rule of George IV, the Prince of Wales who acted as Regent. Antique ornamentation flourished at this time because of the influence of excavations at Pompeii.

The decoration on this tree consists of swags, tassels, miniature mirrors and pierced medallions, stars, lyres, cherubs, and fleur-de-lis, all characteristic of the period. The tree is topped with a Prince of Wales plume of ostrich feathers and needlework. One gold leaf color was used for all the painted ornaments, ribbons, tassels,

cording, and other such detail. The remaining ornamentation was executed in cranberry red, a soft green, and creamy white.

At Christmas, a large beautifully decorated Blue spruce tree becomes the center of attraction in the Great Hall in Carter's Grove. The tree stands on an Oriental carpet and in front of a background of skillfully crafted finely detailed wood paneling, small-paned windows set in deep reveals, built-in window seats, and formal damask draperies hanging in soft folds and trimmed with fringe and tassels. The broad staircase with a spectacular curved banister adds luster to the scene.

The ornaments on the tree are believed to have been ones collected by families who have lived at Carter's Grove. Large silvered kugels of 19th century design are on the floor at the base of the tree and smaller hand-blown glass baubles are intermingled in the branches. Other ornamentation includes paper cornucopias, miniature Victorian parasols and fans, popcorn chains, bead chains, and mini-packages tied with pretty ribbons.

A Crown Center Tree That Grows Ornaments

Crown Center Christmas Tree. Photograph by Mark McCabe

Thousands of people gather annually for the lighting of the Mayor's Christmas tree at Crown Center in Kansas City on the day after Thanksgiving. The hundred-foot Douglas fir tree is cut each year in late October and donated by Willamette Industries in Oregon. To meet the oversized load limits of interstate highways, the branches are pulled toward the trunk and some of the larger ones cut off for reattachment later. A specially made trailer carries the tree on the five day journey of nearly two thousand miles through six states to Kansas City.

After the holidays, the tree is sent to a milling company where it is cut into planks of wood which are used to make two thousand limited edition ornaments. Hallmark Card's artist Fayrol Unverferth has designed many of the commemorative ornaments for past years, a recent one was a three-inch by four-inch laser cut locomotive. In her words, "I chose the locomotive design because when children come to visit the Mayor's Christmas tree, they always remember the toy train under the tree." What is left of the tree after creating the ornaments is recycled as mulch for hiking trails and playgrounds. The money collected from the sale of these ornaments is placed in a fund to serve the city's needy, elderly, and forgotten during the holiday season.

The cut tree after the holidays.

Hallmark artist Fayrol Unverferth

Designing the ornaments.

Making the ornaments.

Photographs courtesy
of Hallmark Cards, Inc.

Crown Center Locomotive

The National Christmas Tree

In 1923, President Calvin Coolidge began the tradition of lighting an outside tree which was initially called the National Community Christmas Tree. A gift from Middlebury College, the fir tree was cut in Coolidge's home state of Vermont, erected on the Ellipse south of the White House, and lit by Coolidge on Christmas Eve. The first living Christmas tree, a large Norway Spruce, was planted in 1924 in Sherman Plaza near the east entrance of the White House, and served as the National Community Christmas Tree for ten years. Special recognition was given to the event the following year in a nation-wide radio broadcast.

During subsequent years both living and cut trees were used. Several trees planted in various locations on the White House grounds did not long survive. A thirty-foot tall Colorado Blue spruce transplanted on the Ellipse in 1978 finally took root and became what is now known as the National Christmas Tree. This tree had been a personal Mother's Day gift to Mrs. William E. Myers and stood on her farm in York, Pennsylvania, for fifteen years. Surrounding the National Christmas Tree in an area known as "The Pathway of Peace" are fifty-seven smaller trees representing the fifty states, the territories, and the District of Columbia.

Except for the top ornament, the lights on the National Christmas Tree remained unlighted in 1979 as a symbolic gesture to honor the Americans held hostage in Iran. For the second year in a row, the tree was not lighted except for 417 seconds, one second for each day the hostages had been held in captivity. On Ronald Reagan's Inaugural Day, January 20, 1981, as the aircraft carrying the former hostages home cleared Iranian airspace the lights went on again. They were turned down momentarily on Christmas Eve of 1985 to recognize American hostages in Lebanon and their families at home.

The presidential lighting of the National Christmas Tree is usually a festive ceremony with thousands of people in attendance and millions more catching a glimpse on television at home. It has become traditional for the First Lady to ride to the top in a hydraulic lift to place a new star ornament on the tree after which the decorating and lighting begins. Customary exhibits include a nativity scene (crèche), reindeer, a Yule log, and in 1994 a model railway display was added. The crèche which had not been shown for nineteen years was reinstated in 1984 after the Supreme Court ruled it to be historically and legally appropriate.

The ceremony is replete with celebrities and entertainers showing off their talents. Headliners during past years have included Jim Nabors, television's Gomer Pyle, Jane Powell, movie actress, Charley Pride and Loretta Lynn of country music fame, and Richard Leech, opera star. The venerable Willard Scott, NBC weatherman, has played the role of Santa Claus for many years.

The National Christmas Tree.

White House Trees

For President John Adams, the first occupant of the White House, a Christmas tree would have been a "politically incorrect" symbol. Christmas was not at all popular and Christmas trees were still seen as an irreligious and pagan symbol. President Franklin Pierce's tree in 1856 was only for family and friends. It was not until 1889 during the administration of President Benjamin Harrison that a White House tree became the official tree. Grover Cleveland was the first to have electric lights on his tree.

President and Mrs. John F. Kennedy and the Blue Room Christmas Tree. Courtesy John Fitzgerald Kennedy Library, Boston, Massachusetts

President and Mrs. Ronald Reagan and the Blue Room Christmas Tree.
Courtesy Ronald Reagan Library, Simi Valley, California

Theodore Roosevelt, the ardent conservationist, forbade a Christmas tree in the White House. His namesake and distant relative, Franklin Roosevelt, who liked to call himself a Christmas tree farmer, had a special liking for beautifully decorated trees at Hyde Park and the White House. Since that time the tree in the Blue Room, decorated by the First Lady, White House staff, and volunteers from throughout the country, has become a tradition. The public is invited and thousands of people come to view its splendor. More than twenty other trees and wreaths at outside windows combine to make Christmas at the White House a truly festive occasion.

Special Themes for Blue Room Trees

First Lady Jacqueline Kennedy began the practice of decorating the Christmas Tree in the Blue Room with a special theme. The ornaments on her tree were crafted to capture the spirit of Tchaikovsky's *Nutcracker* ballet with sugarplum fairies, toy soldiers, candy canes, toy musical instruments, lollipops, and miniature baskets of fruit. Every Christmas since, the First Ladies have created their own special themes and decorative designs for the Blue Room trees.

A Gift from Tree Growers

During the past thirty years White House Christmas trees have been presented by tree growers chosen through a contest held at the convention of the National Christmas Tree Association. Each year the lucky winner travels to Washington, D.C. and has the honor of presenting the tree to the First Lady at the White House.[4] The growers who have provided a Christmas tree for the Blue Room, some of them several times, are listed below:

1966	Howard Pierce, Wisconsin
1967	Gordon Anderson, Ohio
1968	Don Goodwin, Indiana
1969	Roy R. Pierce, Ohio
1970	Calvin J. Frelk, Wisconsin
1971	Kermit Johnson, North Carolina
1972	Alvin Hofert, Washington
1973	Home & Bruner Sides, North Carolina
1974	Ed Cole, Michigan
1975	Guy Cockburn, New York
1976	Ken Guenter, Wisconsin
1977	Alvin Hofert, Washington
1978	Guy Cockburn, New York
1979	Eric & Gloria Sundback, West Virginia
1980	Harry Eby, Indiana
1981	Eric & Gloria Sundback, Pennsylvania
1982	Hal & Sarah Johnson, North Carolina
1983	Ken Scholz, Washington
1984	Hal & Sarah Johnson, North Carolina
1985	Stephen Vander Weide, Michigan
1986	Ron & Dorothy Palmer Charles & Dorothy Burton, Washington
1987	Eric & Gloria Sundback, West Virginia
1988	Irv & Alyce Daggett, Wisconsin
1989	Dwayne, Meade & Bradley Berkey, Pennsylvania
1990	R. Bruce & Michael Lacey, North Carolina
1991	Gary & Audrey Sander, Oregon
1992	Rob Kintigh, Oregon
1993	Wayne Ayers, North Carolina
1994	Lynn & Myron Schmidt, Missouri
1995	Ron Huddler & Danny Dollar, North Carolina
1996	Ken and Joan Scheetz, Ohio
1997	Sanford Fishel, North Carolina

State Capitols and Mansions Light Their Trees

Most of the states display Christmas trees in their capitol rotundas, executive mansions, and sometimes decorate growing trees on the capitol grounds. In South Dakota, a large tree is donated by citizens and brought in by truck to the Great Hall of the State Capitol. The decorations are all hand made by craft groups throughout the State. Oregon features "Holiday at the Capitol" complete with a traditional Douglas fir and a miniature train, a village of historic buildings, and school choral groups singing in the rotunda. Tree lighting ceremonies in Virginia began more than fifty years ago with a live tree on the capitol grounds but in recent years a cut tree from the Virginia Tree Growers Association is displayed.

Louisiana promotes trees grown in the state including the winners of an annual competition sponsored by the Louisiana-Mississippi Christmas Tree Association. From a dozen to three dozen trees are commonly placed in prominent locations throughout the capitol complex in Baton Rouge. Christmas in 1991 was a banner year with fifty-seven trees as a "Salute of the U. S. Armed Forces." Each tree had a unique Louisiana theme and a vast array of lights added Christmas wonder. In another year the tree in the capitol rotunda was decorated with three hundred handmade ceramic masks representing the many cultures of Louisiana.

The large tree in the capitol of West Virginia is decorated with handmade ornaments donated by the vocational rehabilitation center with smaller trees representing various cultures. Some of the dozen trees

Christmas tree, Georgia State Capitol, Atlanta. Photographed by Phyllis B. Kandul, courtesy Office of the Governor

Christmas tree, Wisconsin State Capitol, Madison. Courtesy Office of the Governor

throughout the Governor's Mansion in Wisconsin portray the state's ethnic heritage and agricultural crops. The tree in the capitol rotunda is decorated with miles of garlands and lights along with handcrafted snowflakes sent from nursing homes throughout the state. The annual holiday ceremony in Atlanta, Georgia, is held early in December and features a beautifully decorated twenty-five foot tree in the capital rotunda.

Christmas trees with white lights are displayed outside the State House in Rhode Island at the front and back entrances. On the inside a large tree with brass ornaments stands in the State Room and in the Rotunda there are small trees decorated by various ethnic groups in the state. The trees were donated by the Rhode Island Christmas Tree Growers Association.

Christmas tree, State House, Rhode Island. Courtesy Cynthia Wardwell, Office of the Governor

The twenty-five foot Christmas tree in the Reception Room of the Rhode Island State House with its custom made historical ornaments befits the lavish surroundings. The room was designed in the style of Louis XIV with towering marble pilasters and pink, white, and gold details throughout. The historical theme of the Reception Room is evident in the Gilbert Stuart portrait of George Washington hung over the mantel as well as numerous other pieces of period art and artifacts. Courtesy Cynthia Wardwell, Office of the Governor

Trees for Mansions

The Mansions of Newport

In the last half of the 19th century, Newport, Rhode Island, became the summer social center of the rich and famous. The superb summer climate and a degree of remoteness with miles of sandy coastline caused families of high social status to build elegant and opulent homes. The Preservation Society of Newport County has played a major role in the preservation and maintenance of many of these great houses since those days of splendor.

Chateau Sur Mer

One of the early palatial mansions, Chateau Sur Mer, was built for William Shepard Wetmore who made his fortune with trading and banking companies. This Victorian style home by the sea was the creation of builder Seth Bradford c. 1851-52, and later enlarged by a prominent architect of the day, Richard Morris Hunt. Hunt was educated at the prestigious Ecole des Beaux Arts in Paris and his subsequent assignments in France and Italy influenced the design of this outstanding Newport "cottage" as can be seen in the tall Mansard roof. The size of the ballroom is impressive and was among the first high style French interiors in Newport. The interior has an abundance of ornate Louis XV inspired detail executed by the firm of Leon Marcotte. The photograph shows a paper lantern and strung bead decorated Christmas tree that echoes the mid-19th century mood of the ballroom.

Chateau-sur-mer Ballroom Christmas tree.
Courtesy The Preservation Society of Newport County, Newport, Rhode Island

The Breakers

The largest and most magnificent of the Newport "summer cottages," the Breakers, was built in 1895 for Cornelius Vanderbilt, a grandson of the famous railroad and shipping magnate, and older brother of William Kissam Vanderbilt. The Breakers was the inspiration of architect Richard Morris Hunt, the designer who was responsible for numerous well-known structures in the Middle Atlantic area. The Italian Renaissance Revival home is characterized with arches, loggias, balustrades, a porte-cochere, and hipped roof in the midst of an eleven acre tract of land surrounded by formal gardens, curved roadways, and carved figures to create an aura of dignity and elegance. The interior spaces are even more lavish with ornate paneled walls, crystal chandeliers, massive fireplaces, a sweeping staircase, rich colorful fabrics, and oversize paintings, tapestries, and mirrors. Most of the furnishings are original to the home.

The Christmas tree shown below is in the library, and decorated with an abundance of snow-flakes, strands of pearls, and white lights, a welcomed contrast against the dark paneled walls of black walnut. In the background are glass front bookcases built into the walls, headed with double arches, and upper walls covered with dark green leather with panels of diapering, and an elaborate coffered ceiling. Gilding highlights most areas of the walls and ceiling.

The Breakers Library at Christmas.
Courtesy The Preservation Society of Newport County, Newport, Rhode Island

Hearst Castle

Once the private domain of William Randolph Hearst, the newspaper magnate, Hearst Castle expresses the lifestyles of the wealthy and flamboyant during the 1930's. George Bernard Shaw described it as what God would have built "had he had the money." All of this splendor has since become the public domain of the California Park Service which has opened the doors to tourists with a little cash or credit cards.

In 1922, high on a hill above the Pacific, the first excavations for the Hearst Castle were made. With the labor of a multitude of artisans and vast crews of workers, architect and planner, Julia Morgan created a magnificent estate characteristic of the Mediterranean Revival period. Morgan received her architectural training at the Ecole des Beaux in Paris, as had Richard Hunt, the architect for many of the Newport "cottages." Her first independent commission was a belltower on the Mills College Campus in Oakland which withstood the 1906 earthquake!

The Hearst grounds consist of 127 acres of beautifully landscaped rolling and mountainous terrain which contains expansive gardens, fountains, pools, terraces, esplanades, and vistas embellished with a seemingly endless variety of trees, plants, shrubs, vines, and flowers. Skilled horticulturists and gardeners are employed and five greenhouses replenish the myriads of rhododendrons, azaleas, roses, fuschias, and other flowers so typical of the area. A special fuschia was developed by the first Head Groundskeeper, H. Dodson "Hap" Hazard, and bears his name, the "Hap Hazard" fuschia. Expansive grasslands, stables, and orchards add to the interest and uniqueness of this estate.

In the midst of the grounds and high on a mountain are the main house, *La Casa Grande*, and a number of large and impressive "guest cottages," which are elaborate mansions in and of themselves. There are 38 bedrooms and 41 bathrooms in a house that has 60,645 square feet.

The Castle and cottages are showplaces that bring together historic and decorative architecture, art, antiques, and artifacts, reminiscent of the regal estates of Europe, largely of Italian Renaissance inspiration. Much of the building material as well as the furnishings, which came from many parts of the world, were shipped by tramp steamer to San Simeon Bay, stored in warehouses until needed, and then transported by chain-driven trucks five miles up the mountain side.

Many of the political, literary, and Hollywood faces of the day were entertained by Hearst and his constant companion, movie star, Marion Davies. Some 50-60 guests would intermingle and socialize at the various guest cottages at will. They had a choice of swimming in a Greco-Roman outdoor pool or an indoor pool lined with Venetian glass and gold. Guests might find a bed in which Cardinal Richelieu had slept, a suite in which valuable oil paintings from Italy or Flemish tapestries adorned the walls, or come face-to-face with an authentic suit of armor or interesting antiques placed on top of a trestle table or credenza. Others could admire colorful Navajo rugs or rich Oriental carpets.

The vast Gothic style high ceiling dining room, often referred to as "The Refectory," was furnished with a very long refectory table and heavy Italinate chairs. All this splendor was not without cost. Hearst imposed strict obligations upon his guests. All were expected to rise and dress for breakfast which was served buffet style between 8:00 AM and noon, assemble there before 2:00 PM for lunch, and be prompt for the on-schedule 8:30 PM cocktails and 9:00 PM dinner. The seating order was changed daily.

In spite of the elegant surroundings, the table settings were more reminiscent of a working-class restaurant. There were no tablecloths, centerpieces consisted of condiments such as catsup and mustards in original containers, and homemade preserves. Only paper napkins were used. Following dinner the guests were expected to join Hearst and Marion Davies to watch old movies.

It is traditional that San Simeon be well decorated for the Christmas season. In the Assembly room a single outstanding large tree is the focal point of this 82' by 30' room. In the Refectory, an oversize reproduction of the Nativity scene placed in the musician's loft creates an aura of divinity. Numerous smaller decorated Christmas trees and an abundance of pine boughs on the long tables complete the Christmas decor.

Christmas tree in the Assembly Room, Hearst Castle.
Photograph by John Blades, courtesy Hearst San Simeon State Historical Monument

CHRISTMAS TREE SPECIES IN NORTH AMERICA

The species and subspecies below are listed by their common names which may not be the same in different parts of countries or the world. Their scientific names, which identify them by genus and a qualifying description, are the same everywhere.

Aleppo pine
  Pinus halepensis
Arizona cypress
  Cupressus arizonica var. glabra
Austrian pine
  Pinus nigra var. nigra
Balsam fir
  Abies balsamea
Blue spruce (includes Colorado spruce)
  Picea pungens
Canaan fir
  Abies balsamea var. phanerolepis
Concolor fir (also called White fir)
  Abies concolor
Coastal Douglas fir
  Pseudotsuga menziesii
Deodar cedar
  Cedrus deodara
Eldarica pine (also called Afghan pine)
  Pinus eldarica
Eastern Red cedar
  Juniperus virginiana
Eastern White pine
  Pinus strobus
Fraser fir
  Abies fraseri
Giant redwood
  Sequoiadendron giganteum
Grand fir
  Abies grandis
Leyland cypress
  X cupressocyparis leyandii
Lodgepole pine
  Pinus contorta var. latifolia
Mexican Border pine (actually Southwestern White pine)
  Pinus strobiformis

Monterey pine
  Pinus radiata
Noble fir
  Abies procera
Nordmann fir
  Abies nordmanniana
Norway spruce
  Picea abies
Pacific Silver fir
  Abies amabilis
Pinyon pine
  Pinus edulis
Red pine (also called Norway pine)
  Pinus resinosa
Red spruce
  Picea rubens
Rocky Mountain Douglas fir
  Pseudotsuga menziesii var. glauca
Sand pine
  Pinus clausa
Scotch pine (also called Scot's pine)
  Pinus sylvestris
Serbian spruce
  Picea omorika
Shasta red fir (variety of California Red fir)
  Abies magnifica var. shastesis
Shore pine (variety of Lodgepole pine)
  Pinus contorta var. contorta
Spruce pine
  Pinus glabra
Turkish fir
  Abies bornmuelleriana
Virginia pine
  Pinus virginiana
Western White pine
  Pinus monticola
White spruce (includes Black Hill spruce)
  Picea glauca

87

AMERICAN AND CANADIAN CHRISTMAS TREE INDUSTRY LEADERSHIP

American Officials and Directors

Officers and Directors of the *National Christmas Tree Association* with headquarters in Milwaukee, Wisconsin, 1995-1997

Officers: Bob G. Scott, President, David Stenger, Vice President, Burl Hollingsworth, Secretary/Treasurer, Ann Kirk Davis, Executive Committee, James Corliss, Executive Committee

David E. Baumann, Executive Director, Joan Geiger, Associate Executive Director, Chris Whiting, Administrative Assistant

Present and Past Directors, 1990-1997

John Ahrens, French Armstrong, Will Almedinger, Mitzi Anderson, Herbert Attaway, Waightstill Avery, Jaye Baldwin, Joel Berry, R. H. "Bob" Blair, James Chandler, Leo Clark, James Corliss, Ann Kirk Davis, Ronald Emery, John Feisley, Calvin Frelk, Marvin Gaffney, Frank Gentry, Clarke Gernon, Michael Godzyk, Charlie Grogan, David Hash, Burl Hollingsworth, Robert Housedorf, Dick Jeffery, Dave Jenkins, Keith Jacob, Wayne Korson, John Kreitner, Ira "Bud" Lyon, Stanley Lyon, Betty Malone, B.R. "Bill" Murray, Borden Nanney, Bruce Niedermeier, Ramon Nolte, Clint Pace, Denise Pagura, Gene Potter, Reginald "Reggie" Pulliam, John Scheetz, Don Schiltz, Harold "Hal" Schudel, John Skawinski, Ellis Schmidt, Dean Schnoor, Bob Scott, Dale Shepherd, Theodore Slocum, Clell Soloman, Mark Steelhammer, David Stenger, Chester Stephens, Fred Strathmeyer, Sr., Fred Strathmeyer, Jr., James Thomas, Lloyd Vander Streek, Stephen Vander Weide, Peter Wood, Arthur Yonkey

Executives of State and Regional Associations in the United States, 1997

James Frye, Secretary/Treasurer, *Alabama Christmas Tree Association*; Mike Wade, Executive Director, *California Christmas Tree Growers Association*; John Olsen, Executive Director, *Connecticut Christmas Tree Association*; Debra Harris, Secretary, *Florida Christmas Tree Association*; Paschal Brewer, Secretary/Treasurer, *Georgia Christmas Tree Association*; Janice Brown, Executive Director, *Illinois Christmas Tree Association*; Stan Zaley, Secretary/Treasurer, *Indiana Tree Growers Association*; Carol Jenkins, Secretary, *Inland Empire Christmas Tree Association*; Jan Pacovsky, Executive Secretary, *Iowa Christmas Tree Growers Association*; Sally Wright, Secretary, *Kansas Christmas Tree Growers Association*; Michael May, Executive Secretary, *Louisiana/Mississippi Christmas Tree Association*; Albert Gondeck, Executive Secretary, *Maine Christmas Tree Association*; Andrew Cashman, Secretary, *Maryland Christmas Tree Association*; H. Peter Wood, Executive Director, *Massachusetts Christmas Tree Growers Association*; Laurie Koelling, Executive Director, *Michigan Christmas Tree Association*; Stan Zaley, Executive Administrator, *Mid-America Christmas Trees*; Margaret Michael, Executive Secretary, *Mid-South Christmas Tree Association*; Pat Olive, Executive Director, *Minnesota Christmas Tree Growers Association*; Virgil Kingrey, Secretary, *Missouri Christmas Tree Producers Association*; Rhea Demarais, Secretary/Treasurer, *Montana Christmas Tree Association*; Dixie Heinricks, Secretary/Treasurer, *Nebraska Christmas Tree Growers Association*; Pam Dwyer, Executive Secretary, *New Hampshire/Vermont Christmas Tree Association*; John E. Perry, Executive Secretary, *New Jersey Christmas Tree Growers Association*; Robert Norris, Executive Secretary, *New York Christmas Tree Growers Association*; Patricia Thiel Wilkie, Executive Director, *North Carolina Christmas Tree Association*; Northeast District Forester, *North Dakota Christmas Tree Growers Association*; Rhea Dawn Smith, Executive Director, *Ohio Christmas Tree Association*; Jean Collins, *Oklahoma Christmas Tree Association*; Bryan Ostlund, Executive Secretary, *Pacific Northwest Christmas Tree Association*; Melissa Piper Nelson, Executive Secretary, *Pennsylvania Christmas Tree Growers Association*; Theresa Hayden, Executive Secretary, *Rhode Island Christmas Tree Growers*; Linda Staley, Secretary/Treasurer, *Rocky Mountain Christmas Tree Association*; Marvin Gaffney, Executive Secretary, *South Carolina Christmas Tree Association*; Jim Wilson, Executive Secretary, *Texas Christmas Tree Growers Association*; Katherine Ward, Secretary/Treasurer, *Virginia Christmas Tree Growers Association*; Larry Wilkerson Secretary, *West Virginia Christmas Tree Growers Association*; Virginia Mountford, Executive Secretary, *Wisconsin Christmas Tree Growers Association*; Executive Secretary, *Puerto-Rican-Caribbean Christmas Tree Association*

Canadian Officials and Directors

Officers and Directors of the *Canadian Christmas Tree Growers Association*, 1997

Doug Drysdale, President, Normand Lafreniere, Executive Director, Lewis Downey, Past President

Officers and Directors of Provincial Associations

Jack Wenzell, President, Richard A. Lord, Shawn Lacey, William Stewart, Caryl Warden, ***Christmas Tree Council of Nova Scotia***; Austin Tattrie, Sid Wats, ***Prince Edward Island Christmas Tree Growers Association***, Gordon B. Young, President, L. P. Albert, Secretary, Bill Smith, Bill Hamilton, ***New Brunswick Christmas Tree Growers' Cooperative***; Fernand R. Plante, President, Rock Dufresne, Director General, Christian Morin, Robert E. Enos, Lewis Downey, ***Christmas Tree Growers Association of Quebec***; Jim Turner, President, Gary Thomas, Vice President, Hubert Will, Doug Drysdale, ***Christmas Tree Growers Association of Ontario***; Wane Bilan, President, Art Hoole, Director of Foresty, John McQueen, Canadian Forest Service, ***Manitoba Christmas Tree Growers Association***; Geordie McKay, Executive Director, Henri O'Reilly, Ray Gaudet, Gordon McKay, ***Saskatchewan Christmas Tree Growers Association***

Officers and Directors of the *British Columbia Christmas Tree Council*

Tom Quick, President, Helen Robbins, Secretary, ***Kootenay Christmas Tree Association***; Mike Fleming, President, Diane Gertzen, Recording Secretary, ***Southwest British Columbia Christmas Tree Association***; Bud Collis, President, Betty Collis, Secretary, ***Thompson Okanagan Christmas Tree Association***; Diane Gertzen, P. Ag., Special Projects, Culturist, ***Ministry of Forests, Nursery Extension Services***, Surrey, British Columbia

PICTURE CREDITS

Most of the photographs that appear in the book are credited on the copyright page or as a part of the captions. We would like to thank the families, the choose and cut farms, and others who supplied photographs from their archives and personal collections. The following families were especially generous in this respect: Abraczinskas, Colton, Ehlers, Hofert, Kirk, Musser, Strathmeyer, and Vanden Berg. In addition to those noted in the preface and captions, a number of individuals and organizations deserve special thanks for their assistance in obtaining photographs: Nancy Battis, Crown Center, Kansas City, Missouri; Marcia K. Bullerman, Luther College, Decorah, Iowa; Jøns Dalum, Director, Danish Christmas Tree Producers Association, Frederksberg C, Denmark; Amanda Downs, Social Secretary, British Embassy Washington; David Gerdes, President, Silvaseed Company, Roy, Washington; Clarke J. Gernon, Sr., Shady Pond Tree Farm, Denham Springs, Louisiana; Rita R. Grove, Manager, St. George Tucker House, Colonial Williamsburg Foundation, Williamsburg, Virginia; Reiner Heilmann, Hotel Sacher, Vienna, Austria; Finn Jacobsen, Forest Manager, Langesø Skovbrug, Dyrehavelund 14, Denmark; Raimund Kohl, Gorxheimertal, Germany; Bud Lyons, Lyon's Christmas Trees, Rosemead, California; Stan E. Lock, Deputy Associate Regional Director, National Park Service, U. S. Department of Interior, Washington D.C.; Bryan Ostlund, Executive Secretary, Pacific Northwest Christmas Tree Association; Shirley Riess, The Preservation Society of Newport County, Newport, Rhode Island; Hilary Rinaldi, Hearst Castle, San Simeon, California; Carla Sanders, Office of the Governor, Atlanta, Georgia; Susanne Semmroth and Stefanie Ahlers-Hestermann, Atlantic Hotel, Hamburg, Germany; Governor Tommy G. Thompson, Madison, Wisconsin; Charles Wright, Editor and Publisher, *Christmas Trees*, Lecompton, Kansas. The photograph that appears on page 65 is reprinted from the Winter 1993 edition of *Ampersand*, a publication of Alexander and Baldwin, Inc. Photographs on pages 61 and 62 are credited to Mary Roozeboom, Pella, Iowa.

NOTES

THE BEGINNING IN STRASBOURG

1 In the Eastern Orthodox Churches, Christmas is celebrated on January 7. Gretchen Gesme, who has recently spent several months in St. Petersburg and Moscow, reports that some Russians are now celebrating Christmas on December 25.

2 J. A. Giles, D.C.L., ed., *The Venerable Bede's Ecclesiastical History of England* (London: George Bell & Sons, 1900), p. 56.

3 Otto Lauffer, *Der Weihnachtsbaum in Glauben und Brauch* (Berlin and Leipzig: Walter de Grunter & Co., 1934), pp. 9-10.

4 Ibid., p. 28.

5 Ibid.

6 Josef Ruland, *Christmas in Germany*, 2nd ed., (Bonn: Inter Nationes, 1992), p. 62.

7 Quotation used by Jacob Gilardi, Allersberg bei Nürnberg, a factory for Christmas decorations, sent to the authors by Susanne Schulenburg.

8 For the melodies of the student songs, *Allgemeines Deutsches Commersbuch* (Lahr in Baden, Verlag von Moritz Schauenburg, 1883), p. 224; *The University Song Book* (London: Grant Richards, 9 Henrietta Street, W.C., 1901), pp. 5, 172.

9 A collection of Goliardic poems from the handwritten pages found in the Benediktbeuern monastery was compiled in printed form by J. A. Schmeller in *Carmina Burana* (Stuttgart: Literarischen Vereins, 1847).

10 In 1836, this same German poem was translated into English by Henry Wadsworth Longfellow with the title, *The Hemlock Tree.* Longfellow translated Tannenbaum as hemlock, an evergreen native to North America with which he was familiar.

11 The article, "The Christmas Tree at Windsor Castle," and the drawing of Queen Victoria and family around the tree appeared in *The Illustrated London News, Christmas Supplement, 1848*, pp. 409-410. They are reprinted with permission from The Illustrated London News Picture Library.

12 Ruland, *Christmas in Germany*, pp. 72, 74.

13 From letter dated December 16, 1995, from Alfons Roeck, Leuven, Belgium.

14 Jozef Smosarski, Secretary of the Catholic Monthly *Wiez*, Warsaw, July 1993. Translated by Robert Stryvel.

15 Edward J. Lowell, *The Hessians and the other German Auxiliaries of Great Britain in the Revolutionary War* (Port Washington, N.Y., 1965, originally published in 1884), pp. 2, 3, 20.

16 Germany was divided into literally hundreds of principalities headed by bishops, landgraves, and princes, many of whom were constantly in need of money. The providing of mercenaries was an important source of income.

17 Lowell, *The Hessians*, pp. 88-99; Howard Fast, *The Crossing* (New York: William Morrow and Company, Inc., 1971); William Press Miller, "Victory by Precise Plan," (n.p., n.d.)

18 The Hessian colonel's last name has been spelled as Rall, Rahl, Rohl, and Rhal.

19 Colonel Rahl was likely to have increased the ration of rum for a hearty celebration of Christmas. Two drums of rum were found among the captured Hessian stores by the American victors.

20 Other attacks are reported in a Hessian journal found in Trenton, *Documents Relating to the Revolutionary History of the State of New Jersey*, vol. 1, William S. Stryker, ed., (Trenton: John L. Murphy Publishing Company, 1901), pp. 432-433.

21 Some American authors do not seem to recognize that the primary focus of German Christmas celebration is Christmas Eve, the 24th of December. For example, Howard Fast gives emphasis to the importance of Christmas Day to Germans and does not mention Christmas Eve, *The Crossing*, p. 123. Christmas day is celebrated in Germany but not with the fervor of Christmas Eve. The Second Christmas Day, December 26, the day of Washington's attack, is also a special day for Germans.

22 Rahl spent the night of December 25 at a party given by Tory Abraham Hunt and drank several bumpers of a rum drink and enjoyed a plentiful supply of the best American cuisine. See Fast, *The Crossing*, p. 127. According to English sources of questionable validity, the defeat at Trenton was said to have been caused by the drunkenness of Colonel Rahl. *Revolutionary History*, Stryker, ed., p. 404. Rahl may have been groggy upon awakening but he then took decisive action that almost saved the day for his Hessian forces.

23 Dennis Montgomery, "Renewal and Remembrance," *Colonial Williamsburg*, Journal of the Colonial Williamsburg Foundation, Autumn, 1996, p. 52.

24 Ibid., pp. 49-55.

25 *Canada Weekly*, December 19 and 26, 1979, p. 2.

26 Willi Paul Adams, *The German-Americans, An Ethnic Experience*, American Edition, Translated and Adapted by LaVern J. Rippley and Eberhard Reichmann (Max Kade German-American Center, Indiana University-Purdue University at Indianapolis, 1993), pp. 42-43.

27 Ibid., pp. 2, 4; The Society of Friends, popularly known as Quakers, originated in England. At this time there were approximately 50,000 Quakers in Great Britain but there were also small groups in Ireland, Holland, and Germany.

28 Willa Cather, *My Ántonia* (Boston and New York: Houghton Mifflin Company, 1918), pp. 81-83.

29 L. Dale Ahern, Editor, *Decorah Public Opinion*, wrote a column, "Roadside Ramblings," about the Sellands, January 12, 1944. Additional background information appeared in the *Vesterheim Newsletter*, January, 1968.

A FOCUS ON THE PIONEERS

1 Agnes Carr Sage, "The Christmas Greens of America," *New England Magazine*, New Series, vol. 13; Old Series, vol. 19, September, 1895, February, 1896, pp. 461-465; Alf Evers, *The Catskills* (New York: Doubleday, 1972), pp. 442-443.

2 Phillip V. Snyder, *The Christmas Tree Book* (New York: The Viking Press, 1976), pp. 161-162.

3 Harry Hansen, "The Christmas Tree Ship," in Daniel J. Foley, *The Christmas Tree* (Philadelphia and New York: Chilton Company, 1960), pp. 149-151.

4 From a letter written by D. C. McGalliard, the son of W. V. McGalliard, to the editor of the *American Christmas Tree Growers' Journal*, November, 1960, p. 34.

5 Murray C. Stewart, "Christmas Tree Farming in Indiana County, Pennsylvania," *American Christmas Tree Journal*, vol. 11, no. 4, November, 1967, p. 23.

6 "Biggest Christmas Tree Grower," *Fortune*, December 1952, 140-141.

7 Ibid., 141.

8 The President's wife, Anna Eleanor Roosevelt, was more closely related. President Theodore Roosevelt was her uncle.

9 Speech by Roosevelt at Clarksburg, West Virginia, October 29, 1944 published in *Franklin D. Roosevelt & Conservation, 1911-1945* compiled and edited by Edgar B. Nixon, vol. 2, Hyde Park New York, General Services Administration, National Archives and Records Service, Franklin D. Roosevelt Library, 1957.

10 Nelson C. Brown, "The President Practices Forestry," *Journal of Forestry*, vol. 41, no. 2, February, 1943.

11 President Franklin D. Roosevelt's Personal File, No. 127 contains the letters and memoranda referred to in this section. Made available by Nancy Snedeker, Franklin D. Roosevelt Library.

12 These data were provided by Harold "Hal" Schudel of Holiday Tree Farms, Inc., Corvallis, Oregon.

13 Gary Riessen, "The Future of the Christmas Tree Industry," *American Christmas Tree Journal*, October 1996, pp. 15-21.

14 Bernice McShane, *The Sunday Oklahoman*, July 23, 1995, reprinted in *Christmas Trees*, April 1996, pp. 8, 10.

15 In addition, an estimated 39.6 million American households made use of artificial trees.

CHRISTMAS TREE FORESTS AND FARMS

1 *Christmas Trees*, July 1995, p. 34 and July 1996, p. 38.

2 Donald and Joan Hilliker have written a number of papers on the idea of searching for and adapting new species, for example, "More True Firs for Your Future Success" and "Exotic Firs - A Place in Your Future." Elma, New York: Treehaven Evergreen Nursery, 1995. Bob Girardin has a newsletter, *Exotic News*, and writes feature articles on exotic trees in the *Christmas Trees* magazine.

3 Bob Girardin, "Exotic News," *Christmas Trees*, October, 1995, p. 43 and July, 1996, pp. 50-51.

4 Bob Girardin, "Exotic Update," *Christmas Trees*, January 1996, p. 34.

5 Lewis Hill, *Christmas Trees* (Pownal, Vermont: Storey Communications, Inc. 1989), p. 57.

6 Letter from Paul L. Schroeder, North Countree Christmas, Inc., Wausaukee, WI 54177 in "From the MAILBOX," *Christmas Trees*, July, 1995, p. 6.

7 Hill, p. 97.

CHRISTMAS TREE FORESTS AND FARMS CONTINUED

8 *Christmas Trees*, April 1996, p. 45.

9 Gary Riessen, "Maintaining Tree Freshness," *American Christmas Tree Journal*, April, 1996, p. 5.

10 Mark Owens, "A Tradition of Doing it Yourself," *Christmas Trees*, January, 1996, pp. 12-13.

11 "Christmas Tree Recycling Becomes Part of the St. Louis Landscape," *American Christmas Tree Journal*, April, 1996, page 34.

12 Jeff Bender, "Wauwatosa, Wisconsin, Acting Locally on a Growing Global Problem," *American Christmas Tree Journal*, April, 1996, pp. 36-37.

13 Fran Long, "Christmas Tree Disposal," *Christmas Trees,* October 1996, p. 48.

14 Data provided by Joan Geiger of the National Christmas Tree Association, Milwaukee, Wisconsin.

15 Clarke J. Gernon, Sr., "Growing Exotic Christmas Trees in Louisiana," *Limbs and Needles*, vol. 23, no. 3, Fall 1996, page 13. Published by the North Carolina Christmas Tree Association.

16 The Williams Christmas Tree Farm is operated by the children of Wayne and Ora Mae Williams: Sons Ron and wife Margaret, Don and wife Karen and their sons Bradley, Cory, Tyler, and Joshua, and daughter Laura Bode and husband Gerry.`

17 *Christmas Trees*, January 1996, pp. 31-32.

18 Data provided by Ernesto S. Maurer, *Bosque de los Arboles de Navidad,* Amecameca, Mexico.

19 Jaye and Paul Shereda, who own the Land O'Pines Nursery, began selling trees by mail order in 1988. About one third of their total volume of a thousand trees is sold in this way. The L.L. Bean Company of Freeport, Maine, the Amway Corporation of Ada, Michigan, and Brookstone of Nashua, New Hampshire, list Christmas trees in their catalogs.

20 Relatively few scientific surveys have been conducted in Europe and many trees are sold in a way that precludes statistical tabulation. Some countries such as Sweden and the Czech Republic disclaim any data collection. A problem is that trees from plantations and forests are regulated by different ministries.

21 The Christmas Tree Growers Association of Western Europe (EU) estimates that about fifty million trees are sold annually in Europe. The numbers given for some of the countries and regions are at best rough estimates without the support of scientific surveys. For example, the estimate of eight million trees for eastern Europe includes countries that have little if any data on the subject. For some countries the number of wild trees from forests do not appear to be included in the count. It should also be noted that artificial trees have a lifespan of six or more years which means that the number sold in any one year does not indicate usage.

22 In comparing natural and plastic trees, a Swedish study conducted by the Institute for Air and Environment in Gothenburg used an "Environmental Load Unit" or ELU to measure the strain placed on the environment. The conclusion was that the plastic Christmas tree loads the environment with 20 ELU, while the natural tree only does so with 4.4 ELU.

23 Data received from the Bundesministerium für Ernährung, Landwirtschaft und Forsten, Dr. Gerhard V. Glöy, Agricultural Counselor, Embassy of the Federal Republic of Germany, and through correspondence with Raimund Kohl, Gorxheimertal, Germany. See also Raimund Kohl, "Christmas Trees in Germany," *Christmas Trees*, January 1996, pp. 6-7. The Christmas Tree Growers Association of Western Europe (EU) has estimated that fifteen million trees are sold in Germany annually which includes three million from Denmark and other countries. This number seems far too low. It is unlikely that only 41 percent of German households buy trees compared to 72 percent for Americans.

24 The trees from the forests are harvested by thinning out the tree stands; there is no clear cutting.

25 Raimund Kohl and Ernesto Maurer, "Weed Control with Animals," *Christmas Trees*, January 1996, p. 10.

26 Much helpful information about the growing of Christmas trees in Denmark was provided by Finn Jacobsen, Skovrider, Langesö Skovbrug, Langesøfondet, Dyrehavelund 14, Denmark 5462 Morud and Jøns Dalum, Sektionsleder, Pyntegrøntsektionen, Amalievej 20, Denmark-1875 Frederiksberg C.

27 Data provided by Jens Søgaard Jacobsen of the Danish Christmas Tree Growers Association.

28 The data and other information were provided by Maj-Gen. T. A. Richardson, Secretary of the British Christmas Tree Growers Association and Secretary of the Christmas Tree Growers Association of Western Europe (EU). John H. Godwin, a consultant who resides on the Channel Island of Sark, also supplied helpful facts about the industry in Britain and Europe generally.

29 Data provided by Frédérie Naudet, France, the Christmas Tree Growers Association of Western Europe, and Mme Claudine Emery of the Office National Interprofessionnel des Fruits, des Legumes, et de l'Horticulture (ONIFLHOR), Paris.

30 Data provided by Tormod Stavrum of the Norwegian Christmas Tree Growers Association and the Embassy of Finland.

31 Data provided by Skúli Ólafs, Iceland.

32 Data provided by Bill Murphy, Manager, Coillte Christmas Tree Farms Glenealy, County, Wicklow, Ireland. The Christmas Tree Growers Association of Western Europe has estimated that a million trees are sold annually in Ireland, a number that seems far too high with about a million Irish households.

33 Estimates by the Council of the Christmas Tree Association of Western Europe.

CHRISTMAS TREES IN GLAMOROUS ATTIRE

1 John Tebbel, *George Washington's America* (New York: E.P. Dutton and Company, 1954), p. 62.

2 Carlisle H. Humelsine, "Legacy from the Past," in a book with the same title published by the Colonial Williamsburg Foundation and distributed by Holt, Rinehart and Winston, New York, 1971, pp. 7-16.

3 Ibid. p. 8.

4 A recent presentation is highlighted in an article by Joan Geiger, "Clintons Welcome their Fourth Blue Room Christmas Tree," *American Christmas Tree Journal*, January 1997, pp. 30-31.

SELECT BIBLIOGRAPHY

Books and Articles

Andrews, Clarence. *Christmas in Iowa*. Iowa City, Iowa: Midwest Heritage Publishing Company, 1984.

Barnett, James H. *The American Christmas*. New York: Macmillan, 1954.

Barbara Bush: A Memoir. New York: St. Martin's Paperbacks, 1994.

Carlson, Oliver and Ernest Sutherland Bates. *Hearst, Lord of San Simeon*. New York: The Viking Press, 1936.

Chapman, Arthur G. and Robert D. Wray, *Christmas Trees for Pleasure and Profit*. New Brunswick, New Jersey: Rutgers University Press, 1957.

Colonial Williamsburg Foundation, *Legacy from the Past*, 1971. Distributed by New York: Holt, Rinehart and Winston.

Evers, Alf. *The Catskills, From Wilderness to Woodstock*. New York: Doubleday, 1972.

Fast, Howard. *The Crossing*. New York: William Morrow and Company, Inc., 1971.

Fitzpatrick, John C., ed. *The Dairies of George Washington, 1748-1799 Volume I, 1748-1770; II, 1771-1785; III, 1786-1788; IV, 1789-1799*. Published for The Mount Vernon Ladies Association of the Union, Houghton Mifflin Company, Boston and New York, 1925.

Foley, Daniel J. *The Christmas Tree*. Philadelphia and New York: Chilton Company, 1960.

Goodwin, Doris Kearns. *No Ordinary Time*. New York: Simon & Schuster, a Touchstone Book, 1994.

Hearst, Jr., Mrs. William Randolph. *The Horses of San Simeon*. San Simeon, California: San Simeon Press, 1985.

Hill, Lewis. *Christmas Trees*. Pownal, Vermont: Storey Communications, Inc., 1989.

Hilliker, Jr., Donald B. *Basics of Growing Christmas Trees*. Elma, New York: Treehaven Evergreen Nursery, 1993.

Hupping, Carol. *Let's Celebrate Christmas*. New York: Smithmark Publishers, Inc.,1991.

Johnson, George. *Christmas Ornaments, Lights & Decorations*. Paducah, Kentucky: Collector Books, 1987.

Kocher, A. Lawrence and Howard Dearstyne, *Colonial Williamsburg, Its Buildings and Gardens*. The Colonial Williamsburg Foundation, 1976. Distributed by New York: Holt, Rinehart and Winston.

Lauffer, Otto. *Der Weihnachtsbaum in Glauben und Brauch*. Berlin und Leipzig: Walter de Gruyter & Co., 1934.

Levin, Phyllis Lee. *Great Historic Houses of America*. New York: Coward-McCann, 1970.

Lowell, Edward J. *The Hessians, and other German Auxiliaries of Great Britain in the Revolutionary War*. Port Washington, N. Y., Kennikat Press, Inc., 1965, originally published in 1884.

LemMon, Jean, ed. *An Old-Fashioned Christmas*. Des Moines: Meredith Books, 1992.

Lewis, Jr., Taylor and Joanne Young. *Christmas in New England* New York, Chicago, and San Francisco: Holt, Rinehart and Winston, 1972.

Maguire, Jack. *O Christmas Tree!* New York: Avon Books, 1992.

Metcalfe, Edna, et al. *The Trees of Christmas*. Nashville & New York: Abingdon Press, 1969.

Nonn, Henri. *Strasbourg et sa communaute urbaine*. Paris: La Documentation francaise, 1982.

Pratt, Richard. *Houses, History, and People*. New York: M. Evans and Company, Inc., 1965.

Ringwald, Donald C. *Hudson River Day Line*. New York: Fordham University Press, 1990.

Ruland, Josef. *Christmas in Germany*, Bonn, InterNationes, 1992.

Sage, Agnes Carr. "The Christmas Greens of America." *New England Magazine, 1895*. New Series, vol. 13; Old Series, vol. 19, pp. 461-465. Boston, Mass: Warren F. Kellogg, Publisher.

Selk, Paul. *Mittwinter und Weihnachten in Schleswig-Holstein*. Heide in Holstein: Westholsteinische Verlagsanstalt Boyens & Co., 1972.

Snyder, Phillip V. *The Christmas Tree Book*. New York: Viking Press, 1976; New York: Penguin Books, 1977.

Swanberg, W. A. *Citizen Hearst*. New York: Charles Scribner's Sons, 1961.

Books and Articles continued

Taylor, Jr., Lewis Biggs and Joanne B. Young. *Christmas in Williamsburg*. The Colonial Williamsburg Foundation, Williamsburg, Virginia; distributed by New York: Holt, Rinehart, and Winston, Inc., 1970.

Tebbel, John. *George Washington's America*. New York: E.P. Dutton and Company, Inc., 1954.

Williams, Henry Lionel and Ottalie K. Williams. *Great Houses of America*. New York: G.P. Putnam's Sons, 1966.

Zagarri, Rosemarie, ed. *David Humphrey's "Life of General Washington."* Athens and London: The University of Georgia Press, 1991.

Industry Publications

American Christmas Tree Journal. Milwaukee: National Christmas Tree Association.

Christmas Trees Magazine. Lecompton, Kansas: Tree Publishers, Inc.

Tree Farmer. Washington, D.C.: American Forest Foundation

In the United States and Canada, state and provincial Christmas tree industry associations provide their membership with publications ranging from periodic newsletters to comprehensive quarterly journals.

Videos

The Christmas Tree Story (Blodgett and Corvallis, Oregon: Earthwalker Entertainment and Loma Enterprises). Amye Walker takes the viewer on a journey to find "where Christmas trees come from." Also featured is Harold "Hal" Schudel of the Holiday Tree Farms.

The Messenger of Life: *The Story of the Real Christmas Tree*. The National Christmas Tree Association, Milwaukee, Wisconsin. Produced by Odyssey Productions, Inc., Portland, Oregon. A descriptive video on growing Christmas trees from seed to harvest and the ways in which trees are marketed.

A company video on how Christmas trees are grown including historical background on the early days. The Kirk Company, Tacoma, Washington.

INDEX

Abraczinskas, Andrew, 21, 28

Abraczinskas, Anthony "Duke", 28

Abraczinskas, Evon, 28

Abraczinskas, Margaret, 21

Abraczinskas Nurseries, Inc., 28

Adams, John, President, 77

Agriculture, Department of, 30

Ahl, Ginger, 31

Ahl, John, 31

Albers, Marjorie K., ix

Albert, Prince, 8

Anderson, Gordon, 79

animal damage, 35, 41

Anschutz, Ernest, 7

artificial trees, 45, 50, 55, 57, 59

Atlantic Hotel, Hamburg, 66

Austria, 14, 59, 67

Ayers, Wayne, 79

Barrett, Ronald, 30

Baxter, Bruce, 53

Baxter, Charlotte, 53

Baxter Tree Farm, Afton, New York, 53

Bays, Jim, 38

Bays, Randy, 38

Belgium, 9, 59

Benelux countries, 58, 59

Berkey, Bradley, 79

Berkey, Dwayne, 79

Berkey, Meade, 79

Beutell, Joan, 31

Beutell, Thomas, Jr., 31

Beutell, Thomas, Sr., 31

Bishop, Gary, 32

Boniface, Saint, 3, 6

Breakers (Newport mansion), 83

Britain (England), 8, 9, 10, 12, 58

British Ambassador's Christmas Tree, 66-67

British Christmas Tree Growers Association, 92n

Burton, Charles, 79

Burton, Dorothy, 79

Bush, Barbara, 66

Bush, George, President, 66

Business Week: Kirks featured in, 30-31

Canada, 10, 29, 37, 41, 45; first tree in, 12; industry officials and directors, 89

Carr, Mark, 17, 23

Carter's Grove, 72-73

Cather, Willa, 13-14

Catskill Mountains, 17

Cavaletto, Jackie, 54

Cavaletto, Larry, 54

Chateau-sur-mer (Newport mansion), 82 choose and

cut farms, 39, 51-55; number of, 33, 51; size of, 51

Christ, 3, 14

Christmas: in colonial America, 11; at the Coltons, 64; date of, 3; in Denmark, 9; at Ehlers in Berlin, 63-64; in Finland, 9, 64-65; at Hamilton Field, 63; Hessian celebration of, 10-11; in immigrant homes, 13; papal instructions, 3; and winter solstice, 3, 5; at Vanden Berg family, 61-62

Christmas Eve: German custom, 6, 10, 64

Christmas tree associations: European, 92n, 93n; officials and directors, 88-89; state and regional, 34, 37, 80, 81, 88. *See* National Christmas Tree Association

Christmas tree decorations, 4-5, 6, 61, 64, 65, 69, 76, 79, 80, 81, 82, 83

Christmas tree farms: choose and cut, 33, 51-55; McGalliard as pioneer, 25. *See also* plantations

Christmas Tree Growers Association of Western Europe, 92n, 93n

Christmas tree industry, 15, 33; in Europe, 55-59 (*see also* individual countries); officials and directors, 88-89; size of, 33, 45. *See also* pioneers

Christmas trees: candle lit trees, 4-5, 9, 10, 13, 64; in Colonial America, 11; Colonial Williamsburg, 12, 71-73; in communist Europe, 9, 59; Crown Center, 74-75; decorated tree in 1605, 4; defined, 5-6; divine origin, 4; Ellis Island, 1905, 12; environmentally friendly (*see* recycling); in Europe, 6-7, 8, 9, 55-59, 63-65, 66, 67-69 (*see also* individual countries); exotic trees, 37-38; and German immigrants, 13, 17, 18; growth, rate of, 27, 29, 36, 38, 59; Halifax gift to Boston, 69; Hessian, 11; at home, 6, 61-65; hung from ceiling, 6, 7; as idolatry, 9; in mansions, 82-85; names for, 5; origins of, 3-4; as religious symbol, 5, 7; table top trees, 6, 23; theft of 41, 58; White House, 24, 77-79; at Windsor Castle, 8; worldwide settings, 65-70. *See also* cultivation, harvesting, marketing, planting, species

Christmas tree ships, 30, 65; Hawaiian market, 29-30; Pearl Harbor incident, 29; Schuenemann brothers, 18; sinking of, 18

Churchill, Winston, Christmas tree from F.D.R., 28

Cleveland, Grover, President, 77

climate, 36, 42

cloning, 37

Cockburn, Guy, 79

Cole, Ed, 79

College of William and Mary, 72

Collins, Jean, 33

Cologne Cathedral, 7

Colonial America: Christmas not observed, 11
Colonial Williamsburg: Great Hall tree, Carter's Grove 72-73; Regency tree, Williamsburg Inn, 71, 73; St. George Tucker House, 11, 12, 73
Colton family, 64
computers, use of, 45
conifers, 35; cones, 36; exotic trees, 37-38; seed, 36, 37
conservation, 4, 24, 25; Christmas trees banned in White House, 24, 77, 79; Pinchot, Gifford, 24, 25. *See also* recycling Christmas trees
Coolidge, Calvin, President, 76
Crown Center, 74-75
Crown Zellerbach Company, 32, 33
cultivation: bare soil, 38; climate, 36; equipment, 39, 40, 41; fertilizer, 38, 40; herbicides, 38; pesticides, 40; in sod, 38; soil types, 29, 36, 38
Czech Republic, 9, 59
Daggett, Alyce, 79
Daggett, Irv, 79
Dale, Dwayne, 54
Dalum, Jøns, 26n, 119
Danish Christmas Tree Growers Association, 92n
Davies, Marion, 84
Davis, Ann Kirk, 22
Denmark, 9, 38, 58, 59
disease, 40
Dollar, Danny, 79
Douglas Fir Christmas Tree Company, Shelton, Washington, 33
Eby, Harry, 79
Ehlers family, 63-64
Ehlers, Katrine, 63
Elizabeth II, Queen, 66
Emerald Christmas Tree Farm, Bellevue, Washington, 31
environment. *See* recycling
equipment, 39, 40, 41, 43, 44
Europe, 55-59; plantations, 57, 58, 59; wild trees, 55, 57, 58, 59. *See also* individual countries
Finland, 9, 55, 59, 65
Fishel, Sanford, 79
Fisher, Dorothy, 43
Fleck, Erin, 31
Fleck, Jack, 31
Fleck, Mary Ann, 31
Fleck, Meaghan, 31
France, 7, 8, 59
Frelk, Arlene, 31, 41
Frelk, Calvin, 31, 79
Frelk, George, 31
Geiger, Joan, ix, 92n, 93n
Germany, ix, 5, 7, 8, 9, 12, 13, 27, 55, 57, 59, 63-64
Gernon, Clarke J., Sr., 52, 67
Gesme, Gretchen, 90n

Ginnis, Margaret, 21
Girardin, Bob, 37, 91n
Glöy, Gerhard V., 92n
Godwin, John H., 93n
Goodmonson, Paul, 31, 32
Goodwin, Don, 79
Goodwin, W. A. R., Reverend Dr., 71
greenery: as pagan, 3
Gregory I, Pope, 3
Guenter, Ken, 79
Hallmark Cards, Inc. 75
Hamilton Field, 63
Harrison, Benjamin, President, 77
Harvard University, 71
harvesting: equipment, 43, 44; cutting trees, 43, 44; helicopters, 43, 45: storage, 43; tagging and grading, 20, 42, 43, 44; time for, 42-43
Hawaii, 29-30, 65
Hearst Castle, 84-85
Hearst, William Randolph, 84
Heater, Jim, 43, 44
Helferts Hof, 56, 57
helicopters, 43, 45
Henricks, Fran, 54
Henricks, Steve, 54
Henry, Patrick, 73
Herbert Hoover Presidential Library and Museum, ix
Hessians: celebrate Christmas, 10; early Christmas trees, 11; Trenton, battle of, 10-11
Hill, Lewis, 39, 41
Hilliker, Donald, 91n
Hilliker, Joan, 91n
Hofert, Alvin, 18, 29, 31, 79
Hofert, John A., 29
Hofert, John H., 18, 29
Hofert, Milton, 29
Hoffman, Dan, 41, 42
Hoffman Family Farms, Beavercreek, Oregon, 31
Hoffman, Julie, 31
Hoffman, Robert, 31
Hoffman, Steven, 31
Hoffman Tree Farm, Cedar Rapids, Iowa, 64
Holiday Tree Farms, Inc., Corvallis, Oregon, 32
Howe, Sir William, 10
Hough, Walter and Marion, 63
Huddler, Ron, 79
Hungary, 59
Iceland, 59
insects, 40
Inter Nationes, Bonn, Germany, ix
Ireland, 9, 59
Italy, 9, 59
Jacobs, Keith, 35, 46
Jacobsen, Finn, 92n

Japan, 66
Jefferson, Thomas, President, 73
Jensen, Daniel, ix
J. Hofert Company, 18, 20, 23, 29, 31, 55
Johnson, Hal, 79
Johnson, Kermit, 79
Johnson, Sarah, 79
Kennedy, President John F. and Mrs., 77, 79
Kintigh, Bob, 79
Kirby, Peg, 54
Kirby Tree Farm, Toddville, Iowa, 54
Kirk Company, 21-23, 25, 29, 30, 31, 41, 55, 95
Kirk, Dorothy Fisher, 22
Kirk, George Ridgway "G. R.", 19, 20, 21, 22, 30, 31
Kirk, Morris L. "Mac", 22
Kirk, Paul R. "Rick", Jr., ix, 22, 29
Kirk, Paul Ridgway, Sr., 21, 22, 23, 25, 29, 30, 31
Kohl, Raimund, 57, 92n
Kroeker, Henry, 41
Kroeker, Phyllis, 41
labor, 44-45; training of, 44
Lacey, Michael, 79
Lacey, R. Bruce, 79
Land O'Pines Nursery, Custer, Michigan, 55
Langesø Estate, 57, 58
Lauffer, Otto, 3
Lithuania, 21
Litzinger, Karl, 55
Long, Fran, 51
Louisiana-Mississippi Christmas Tree Association, 80
Luther College, 67
Luther, Martin, 5, 6, 7, 9, 67; mythical Christmas tree, 3, 5, 6; painting by Carl A. Schwerdgeburth, 3
McGalliard, W. V., 25
mail order trees, 55
Maine Christmas Tree Association, 37
managerial/administrative, 44; computers, use of, 45
Manners Christmas Tree Farm, New Lyme, Ohio, 44
mansions, Christmas trees in: 61, 82-85; Hearst Castle, 84; Newport mansions, 82-83
Mardi Gras tree, 67
marketing, 19, 22, 23, 38, 45; and baby boomers, 33; choose and cut, 33, 51-55; early markets, 17-18, 35; mail order, 55; Los Angeles team tracks, 19, 21, 22, 32; prices, 25, 45, 57, 58
Mathisen Tree Farms, Greenville, Michigan, 33, 42
Matson Navigation Line, 30
Maurer, Ernesto S., 55, 92n
Merry Christmas Tree Farm, Tomball, Texas, 44, 53-54
Mexico, 45, 55
Minnigerode, Charles, 11, 71, 72, 73

Montana, Joe, 54
Murphy, Bill, 93n
Murray, Bill, 38
Musser Forests, Inc., Indiana, Pennsylvania, 25-26
Musser, Fred, Jr., 26
Musser, Fred, Sr., 25, 26, 27
Musser, Nancy, 26
mutation, 38; Leyland cypress, 38
Myers, Mrs. William E., 76
National Christmas Tree: ceremonies and celebrities, 76; Willard Scott as Santa, 76
National Christmas Tree Association, ix, 34, 40, 79, 88, 92n
natural trees. *See* wild trees
Nelson, Gary, 29
Neymeyer, Robert, ix
Noble Mountain Tree Farm, Salem, Oregon, 32, 43
Noël Christmas Tree Farm, Santa Barbara, California, 51, 54
Northern Christmas Trees and Nursery, Merrillan, Wisconsin, 31
Norway, 9, 14, 15, 59
Norwegian Christmas Tree Growers Association, 93n
nurseries, 37
O Christmas Tree, 7
Ólafs, Skúli, 93n
O Tannenbaum, middle age melody, 7
Palmer, Dale, 30
Palmer, Dorothy, 79
Palmer, Ron, 79
Paradise tree, 3, 5
personnel. *See* labor
Peste, Fred, 32, 33
Pierce, Franklin, President, 77
Pierce, Howard, 79
Pierce, Roy R., 79
Pinchot, Gifford, 24, 25
pioneers, 17-23, 25, 31-33
plantations, 25-29, 31-33, 35-36, 39; and conservation, 25; early years, 25; in Europe, 55-59; Helferts Hof (Germany), 56, 57; size of, 33
planting, 38, 44; in bare soil, 38; by hand, 39; with machine, 39; in sod, 38; spacing, 25, 27, 39
planting stock. *See* nurseries, plugs, seed, seedlings, transplants
Plog, William, Hyde Park Superintendent, 27, 28
plugs, 37
Poland, 9, 59
Portugal, 9, 59
Prairie Pines Christmas Tree Farm, Wichita, Kansas, 51
prices, 25, 45, 57, 58
Prudential Center, Boston: tree from Halifax, 69
pruning, 35, 41, 42

quality, 35-38; cloning, 37; mutation, 38
Rahl, Johann Gottlieb, Colonel, 10, 11
Reagan, President Ronald and Mrs., 76, 78
recycling Christmas trees, 46, 50-51; in Europe, 55;
    number recycled, 51
Rhode Island Christmas Tree Growers Association,
    81
Richardson, T. A., Major General, 92n
von Riedesel, Friedreich Adolph, Major General, 12
Riessen, Gary, 33, 37
Roberts, Ruth, 33
Rockefeller, John D. Jr., 72
Roosevelt, Archie, 24
Roosevelt, Eleanor, 28
Roosevelt, Franklin Delano, President, 27-28, 29, 35
Roosevelt, Quentin, 24
Roosevelt, Theodore, President, 24, 25, 27, 79
Roth, Hella, ix
Russia, 9, 59
Sacher Hotel, Vienna, 67-69
Sander, Audrey, 79
Sander, Gary, 79
Santa Claus, 52, 62, 64, 69, 76; other names for, 61,
    64, 65
Scandinavia, 8, 13, 25
Schaefer, Robert, 32, 43
Scheetz, Joan, 79
Scheetz, Ken, 79
Schmidt, Lynn, 79
Schmidt, Myron, 79
Scholz, Ken, 79
Schroeder, Paul, 39
Schudel, Harold "Hal", 29, 31-32, 95
Schuenemann, August, 18
Schuenemann, Herman, 18
Schwerdgeburth, Carl A., 3
Scott, Bob, ix, 40, 43, 51
Scott, Esther, 29
Scott, Jack, 44, 53
Scott, Janie, 44, 53
Scott, Lyall F., 29
Scott, Scott C., 29
Scott, Willard, 76
seed, 36, 37; orchards, 27, 37. *See also* cloning,
    seedlings
seedlings, 1, 36-37, 39. *See also* plugs, transplants
Selland, Anna, 14-15
Selland, Erick, 14-15
Shady Pond Tree Farm, Pearl River, Louisiana, 52
shearing, 21, 35, 41, 44; equipment, 41; in Europe,
    55, 57, 58; number sheared, 41-42; wild trees, 25,
    35
Shepherd, Dale, 33
Shepherd, Ruth, 33
Shereda, Jaye, 92n

Shereda, Paul, 92n
Sides, Bruner, 79
Sides, Home, 79
Silver Mountain Christmas Trees, Sublimity,
    Oregon, 43
Spain, 9, 59
species, 35, 36, 46, 87; map showing popular
    species, 47;   photographs of, 48-49;
Sports Center Christmas Tree Farm, Topeka,
    Kansas, 54
sprayers and spraying, 40, 44
State capitols and mansions, 80-81
Stewart, Murray, 25
Stohr, Billy, 32
Stohr, Brandt, 32
Stohr, Clarence, 32
Stohr, Joy, 32
Stohr, Robert Clarence, 32-33
Stohr, Stephanie, 32
Strasbourg: decorated tree in 1605, 4; profusion of
    trees, 8
Strathmeyer, Brian, 27
Strathmeyer, Charles H., 20
Strathmeyer, Charles W., 19, 26, 27
Strathmeyer Forests, Inc., Dover, Pennsylvania, 26-
    27
Strathmeyer, Fred, Jr. 27
Strathmeyer, Fred, Sr. 27, 51
Strathmeyer, Gerrit, 27
Strathmeyer, Robin, 27
Strathmeyer, Tim, 27
stump culture, 39-40
stumps: removal of, 44
Sundback, Eric, 66, 79
Sundback, Gloria, 66, 79
Sweden, 59
Swift, Dean, 37
Switzerland, 18, 59
Taylor, Ruth, 44
theft: 41, 58
transplants, 36, 37, 39. *See also* seedlings
Treehaven Evergreen Nursery, Elma, New York, 91n
Tucker, Nathaniel Beverley, Judge, 11, 12, 72
Tucker, St. George, 12
Tully, Grace G., F.D.R. secretary, 28
Unverferth, Fayrol, Hallmark artist, 75
Vanden Berg family, 61, 62
Vanderbilt, Cornelius, 83
Vander Weide, Stephen, 79
Vesterheim Norwegian-American Museum,
    Decorah, Iowa, 15, 69-70
Victoria, Queen, 8, 58
Wahmhoff, Carl, 33
Wahmhoff Farms, Gobles, Michigan, 33
WAL-MART, 45

Warren, Buzz, 54

Warren, Janet, 54

Warren Plantation, Stanley, Kansas, 44

Washington, George, 10, 11, 71, 72, 73

White House Christmas trees, 61; Blue Room trees, 78-79; Christmas trees banned, 24, 77, 79; in closet, 24; special themes, 79; tree growers as contributors, 79

wild tree plantations, 23, 25, 29, 32

wild trees, 17, 18, 19, 24, 33, 35, 55, 57

Williams, Bill, 30

Williams, Karen, 54

Williamsburg, 11, 71, 72. *See also* Colonial Williamsburg

Williams Tree Farm, Rockton, Illinois, 54

Windsor Castle, 8

Wolf Creek Tree Farm and Nursery, Tuckasegee, North Carolina, 31

Worthington, Earl, 37

Young, Howard, 50

Yule Tree Farms, Aurora, Oregon, 43

Zarnack, August, 7